FLORIDA TEST PREP

Persuasive Writing Workbook

A Complete Guide to Writing Opinion Pieces

Grade 5

© 2018 by F. Hawas

All rights reserved. No part of this book may be reproduced or transmitted in any form or by any means, electronic, mechanical, photocopying, recording, or otherwise without prior written permission.

ISBN 978-1724887078

TEST MASTER PRESS

www.testmasterpress.com

CONTENTS

Practice Sets: Developing Writing Skills   **5**

    Warm-Up Exercise: Best and Worst Qualities   6
Set 1: Stating an Opinion   8
    Warm-Up Exercise: Using Sequence Words   14
Set 2: Organizing Your Ideas   15
    Warm-Up Exercise: Pros and Cons   20
Set 3: Listing and Choosing Supporting Ideas   22
    Warm-Up Exercise: Stating Main Ideas   27
Set 4: Introducing the Topic   29
    Warm-Up Exercise: Choosing a Title   35
Set 5: Starting Strong   37
    Warm-Up Exercise: Using Concrete Details   48
Set 6: Using Details to Support an Opinion   50
    Warm-Up Exercise: Choosing a Topic   55
Set 7: Using Examples to Support an Opinion   57
    Warm-Up Exercise: Personal Experiences and Meaning   62
Set 8: Using Personal Experience to Support an Opinion   64
    Warm-Up Exercise: Using Linking Words and Phrases   69
Set 9: Using Facts to Support an Opinion   70
    Warm-Up Exercise: Introducing the Conclusion   75
Set 10: Writing the Conclusion   76
    Warm-Up Exercise: Using Strong Language   81
Set 11: Using Calls to Action   82

Practice Sets: Applying Writing Skills   **87**

Set 12: Write an Opinion Essay   89
Set 13: Write a Letter   97
Set 14: Write in Response to a Quote   105
Set 15: Write an Article   113
Set 16: Write a Letter to the Editor   121
Set 17: Write a Review   129
Set 18: Write a Research Piece   137
Set 19: Writing to Promote   145
Set 20: Write a Response to Literature   153
Set 21: Write a Response to Informational Texts   168

Writing Review and Scoring Guide   **184**

INTRODUCTION
For Parents, Teachers, and Tutors

This workbook will develop strong persuasive writing skills and give students the ability to write effective opinion pieces of all types. The first section will develop the essential persuasive writing skills one by one. The second section allows students to apply these skills and gives students practice creating a wide range of opinion pieces.

By completing the writing tasks in this book, students will be able to create writing that meets the requirements listed in the state standards and respond effectively to all types of writing prompts.

State Standards for Writing

The Language Arts Florida Standards (LAFS) divide writing skills based on text type and purpose. The three types of writing are opinion pieces, informative/explanatory texts, and narrative writing. This book focuses on opinion pieces, and has been specifically created to develop the skills listed in the standards. The exercises and tasks will develop all the skills described in the standards and ensure that students are able to write opinion pieces with the key characteristics expected.

Section 1: Developing Writing Skills

The first section of the book contains 11 sets of exercises and prompts. Each set is focused on one key element of persuasive writing. The first task in each set introduces the skill and guides students through the task. Students then master the skill by completing the four additional writing tasks. Each set also includes a warm-up exercise to prepare students for the set, to introduce and develop a key skill needed to complete the task well, or to help students focus on a key feature of persuasive writing.

Section 2: Applying Writing Skills

The second section of the book contains ten sets of writing prompts. Each set is focused on one style or one genre of persuasive writing. Students will use the key elements of persuasive writing and apply the skills they have learned. Hints and tips are also included throughout the section to guide students. As well as developing general writing skills, this section will prepare students for the types of writing tasks found on assessment tasks and tests.

Preparation for the State Tests

Beginning in grade 4, students complete an FSA ELA Writing test each year. The test may include either an opinion writing task or an informative/explanatory writing task. For the opinion writing task, students will write an opinion piece after reading passages. This workbook will help prepare students for the test by teaching students to write opinion pieces with all the features expected of student writing and that meet the key criteria used to score student work. The writing tasks in Set 21 also provide an experience similar to that found on the real tests.

Developing Writing Skills

The exercises in this section will develop the writing skills needed to produce all types of opinion pieces. Each set focuses on developing one specific skill.

Follow the instructions for each writing prompt. Write your answers in the space provided.

For tasks that require complete opinion pieces, a table is included for planning the opinion piece. Plan your work by completing the table. Then write or type an opinion piece of 1 to 2 pages.

Warm-Up Exercise: Best and Worst Qualities

A simple opinion piece can tell the best or worst quality of a person, a place, or an object. Complete each statement by listing the best or worst quality. Then write a paragraph explaining why.

1 My best quality is _____.

_____

_____

_____

_____

2 The best thing about the city or town I live in is _____

_____.

It is the best thing because _____

_____

_____

_____

_____

3 The best thing about winter is _____

_____.

It is the best thing because _____

_____

_____

_____

_____

4 The worst thing about the Internet is _____

_____.

It is the worst thing because _____

_____

_____

_____

_____

Set 1: Stating an Opinion

An opinion piece is a piece of writing that tells what you believe about something. The first step in writing an opinion piece is to clearly state what your opinion is. This is the main idea of your opinion piece. To make people agree with you, you'll also need to explain why you have that opinion.

Read the plan and the short opinion piece below. It gives an example of how to state an opinion and support it. Then practice stating an opinion and supporting it by completing the exercises.

Main Idea: State the main opinion.
You should save half your allowance.
→ Start the opinion piece by writing a sentence or two stating the main idea.
Supporting Ideas: Explain why you have that opinion.
You can save up for something more costly. You'll have extra money when you need it.
→ Write a few sentences explaining why you have that opinion.

Many people receive their allowance, spend it quickly, and have nothing left over. It is better if you get in the habit of always saving half. One reason for saving is that the money adds up and you can then afford even better items. I've bought many things after saving for weeks. It is a great feeling to finally get something you really wanted. The second reason for saving is that you will always have some money ready for a time when you need it. For both those reasons, it is great to make saving a habit.

Writing Prompt 1

State your main idea by completing the statement below. Then describe your supporting ideas by completing the statement.

Main Idea: State the main opinion.
The most inspiring person I know is _____.
→ Start the opinion piece by writing a sentence or two stating the main idea.
Supporting Ideas: Explain why you have that opinion.
He or she is inspiring because _____
_____
_____
→ Write a few sentences explaining why you have that opinion.

Use the plan above to write a short opinion piece.

_____

_____

_____

_____

_____

_____

_____

Writing Prompt 2

State your main idea by completing the statement below. Then describe your supporting ideas by completing the statement.

Main Idea: State the main opinion.
The most exciting types of movie to watch are _____.
→ **Start the opinion piece by writing a sentence or two stating the main idea.**
Supporting Ideas: Explain why you have that opinion.
They are exciting because _____   _____   _____
→ **Write a few sentences explaining why you have that opinion.**

Use the plan above to write a short opinion piece.

_____

_____

_____

_____

_____

_____

_____

Writing Prompt 3

Do you think it is better to buy books or to borrow them from a library?

Use the table below to plan an opinion piece that tells how you feel and why.

Main Idea: State the main opinion.   → **Start the opinion piece by writing a sentence or two stating the main idea.**
Supporting Ideas: Explain why you have that opinion.   → **Write a few sentences explaining why you have that opinion.**

Use the plan above to write a short opinion piece.

_____

_____

_____

_____

_____

_____

_____

Writing Prompt 4

What do you think is an interesting hobby to have?

Use the table below to plan an opinion piece that tells how you feel and why.

Main Idea: State the main opinion.
→ Start the opinion piece by writing a sentence or two stating the main idea.
Supporting Ideas: Explain why you have that opinion.
→ Write a few sentences explaining why you have that opinion.

Use the plan above to write a short opinion piece.

_____

_____

_____

_____

_____

_____

_____

Writing Prompt 5

Many people today write and send a lot of text messages. Do you think this is harming writing skills?

Use the table below to plan an opinion piece that tells how you feel and why.

Main Idea: State the main opinion.
→ Start the opinion piece by writing a sentence or two stating the main idea.
Supporting Ideas: Explain why you have that opinion.
→ Write a few sentences explaining why you have that opinion.

Use the plan above to write a short opinion piece.

_____

_____

_____

_____

_____

_____

_____

Warm-Up Exercise: Using Sequence Words

Words that show the sequence of ideas will keep your work organized and flowing well from one idea to the next. Practice using sequence words by writing a short paragraph that answers each question. In each paragraph, give three reasons to explain why. Use the three sequence words or phrases listed in your paragraph. Be sure to use them in an order that makes sense.

1 Who do you enjoy spending time with? Why do you enjoy it?

        Finally,   For one thing,   As well as that,

_____

_____

_____

_____

2 What do you enjoy doing in your spare time? Why do you enjoy it?

        Additionally,   To begin with,   Lastly,

_____

_____

_____

_____

Set 2: Organizing Your Ideas

Writing Prompt 6

A good opinion piece should be organized well. The plan below shows a common structure of an opinion piece. The first paragraph introduces the topic and states the main idea. The next three paragraphs each focus on one reason for the opinion or one supporting idea. The final paragraph is the conclusion.

Use the plan below to write an opinion piece.

Introduction: Introduce the topic and state the main opinion.
The classrooms at school should be painted yellow.
→ Write a few sentences that tell what the topic is and state the main idea.
Supporting Idea 1: Describe the first reason that supports the opinion.
The old brown color looks dull and dirty. It needs a fresh new color.
→ Write a paragraph focused on the first supporting idea.
Supporting Idea 2: Describe the second reason that supports the opinion.
A nice yellow color would make the classrooms feel cheerful. Students would be in a better mood.
→ Write a paragraph focused on the second supporting idea.
Supporting Idea 3: Describe the third reason that supports the opinion.
The yellow color would be brighter. It would help stop students from feeling tired and sleepy.
→ Write a paragraph focused on the third supporting idea.
Conclusion: Restate the main opinion and finish off the opinion piece.
The color of the classrooms should be changed to yellow.
→Write a paragraph that concludes your opinion piece.

Writing Prompt 7

Think of a job that you think would be rewarding. Write an opinion piece that argues that the job would be rewarding. Be sure to include three reasons that the job would be rewarding to support the opinion.

Use the table below to plan your work. Then write or type your opinion piece.

Introduction: Introduce the topic and state the main opinion.   → Write a few sentences that tell what the topic is and state the main idea.
Supporting Idea 1: Describe the first reason that supports the opinion.   → Write a paragraph focused on the first supporting idea.
Supporting Idea 2: Describe the second reason that supports the opinion.   → Write a paragraph focused on the second supporting idea.
Supporting Idea 3: Describe the third reason that supports the opinion.   → Write a paragraph focused on the third supporting idea.
Conclusion: Restate the main opinion and finish off the opinion piece.   →Write a paragraph that concludes your opinion piece.

Writing Prompt 8

Do you think all students should be required to play a sport? Write an opinion piece explaining why or why not. Be sure to include three reasons to support the opinion.

Use the table below to plan your work. Then write or type your opinion piece.

Introduction: Introduce the topic and state the main opinion.   → Write a few sentences that tell what the topic is and state the main idea.
Supporting Idea 1: Describe the first reason that supports the opinion.   → Write a paragraph focused on the first supporting idea.
Supporting Idea 2: Describe the second reason that supports the opinion.   → Write a paragraph focused on the second supporting idea.
Supporting Idea 3: Describe the third reason that supports the opinion.   → Write a paragraph focused on the third supporting idea.
Conclusion: Restate the main opinion and finish off the opinion piece.   →Write a paragraph that concludes your opinion piece.

Writing Prompt 9

Think of a place that you think would be a good place for your class to go on a field trip. Write an opinion piece explaining why the class should visit the place. Be sure to include three reasons to support the opinion.

Use the table below to plan your work. Then write or type your opinion piece.

Introduction: Introduce the topic and state the main opinion.   → Write a few sentences that tell what the topic is and state the main idea.
Supporting Idea 1: Describe the first reason that supports the opinion.   → Write a paragraph focused on the first supporting idea.
Supporting Idea 2: Describe the second reason that supports the opinion.   → Write a paragraph focused on the second supporting idea.
Supporting Idea 3: Describe the third reason that supports the opinion.   → Write a paragraph focused on the third supporting idea.
Conclusion: Restate the main opinion and finish off the opinion piece.   →Write a paragraph that concludes your opinion piece.

Writing Prompt 10

Do you think students should have to wear school uniforms? Write an opinion piece explaining why or why not. Be sure to include three reasons to support the opinion.

Use the table below to plan your work. Then write or type your opinion piece.

Introduction: Introduce the topic and state the main opinion.   → Write a few sentences that tell what the topic is and state the main idea.
Supporting Idea 1: Describe the first reason that supports the opinion.   → Write a paragraph focused on the first supporting idea.
Supporting Idea 2: Describe the second reason that supports the opinion.   → Write a paragraph focused on the second supporting idea.
Supporting Idea 3: Describe the third reason that supports the opinion.   → Write a paragraph focused on the third supporting idea.
Conclusion: Restate the main opinion and finish off the opinion piece.   →Write a paragraph that concludes your opinion piece.

Warm-Up Exercise: Pros and Cons

An opinion piece tells what you think about a topic. You can often argue either way. The reasons that are for something are the pros. The reasons that are against something are the cons. Think about each question asked below. Then complete the table by listing pros and cons.

1. Is it good to get up really early on school mornings?
   List good things about getting up really early in the pros column. List bad things about getting up really early in the cons column.

Pros	Cons
You don't feel rushed in the morning.	*You might wake up other people.*

2. Do cats make good pets?
   List good things about keeping cats as pets in the pros column. List bad things about keeping cats as pets in the cons column.

Pros	Cons

3 Is playing computer games good for young people?
List ways that playing computer games is good for people in the pros column.
List ways that playing computer games is bad for people in the cons column.

Pros	Cons

4 Is winter the best season?
List good things about winter in the pros column. List bad things about winter in the cons column.

Pros	Cons

Set 3: Listing and Choosing Supporting Ideas

Writing Prompt 11

A strong opinion piece has good supporting ideas. However, the key is to have a few supporting ideas and explain each one well. You might be able to think of many supporting ideas, but don't try to include all of them. Instead, choose the two or three ideas you think are the most important. Then focus on those.

Practice thinking of reasons to support an opinion by listing five supporting ideas for the opinion below.

Opinion: It is better to play a team sport than an individual sport.

- [ ] *Your teammates support and encourage you.*
- [ ] _____
- [ ] _____
- [ ] _____
- [ ] _____

Select the idea you think is most important. Use the idea you selected to write a few sentences supporting the opinion.

_____
_____
_____
_____

Writing Prompt 12

Think of someone you know who you think would make a good role model for young people. Complete the sentence below to describe your choice. Then list four reasons you think this person would make a good role model.

Opinion: I think _____ **would make a good role model.**

☐ _____

☐ _____

☐ _____

☐ _____

Select the idea you think is most important. Use the idea you selected to write a paragraph supporting the opinion. Make sure your paragraph stays focused on the supporting idea you have chosen.

_____

_____

_____

_____

_____

Writing Prompt 13

List five supporting ideas for the opinion below.

Opinion: Being a successful sportsperson would give you an exciting life.

☐ _____

☐ _____

☐ _____

☐ _____

☐ _____

Select the idea you think is most important. Use the idea you selected to write a paragraph supporting the opinion. Make sure your paragraph stays focused on the supporting idea you have chosen.

_____

_____

_____

_____

_____

_____

Writing Prompt 14

Cell phones today do much more than just allow people to make and receive calls. Think about all the things you can do with a cell phone. Then list four supporting ideas for the opinion below.

Opinion: Cell phones are handy tools that make life easier.

☐ _____

☐ _____

☐ _____

☐ _____

Select the idea you think is most important. Use the idea you selected to write a paragraph supporting the opinion. Make sure your paragraph stays focused on the supporting idea you have chosen.

_____

_____

_____

_____

_____

Writing Prompt 15

List five supporting ideas for the opinion below.

Opinion: Going to camp teaches people important life skills.

☐ _____

☐ _____

☐ _____

☐ _____

☐ _____

Select the idea you think is most important. Use the idea you selected to write a paragraph supporting the opinion. Make sure your paragraph stays focused on the supporting idea you have chosen.

_____

_____

_____

_____

_____

Warm-Up Exercise: Stating Main Ideas

Every introduction should include a sentence that states what the opinion or the main idea is. There are many ways you can introduce the opinion. For each list of topics below, circle a topic that interests you. Then complete each sentence to give three or four opinions you have on the topic.

1   cartoons   reality television   science fiction

I believe that _____

_____.

I feel that _____

_____.

I am sure that _____

_____.

2   pop music   country music   rap music

In my opinion, _____

_____.

In my view, _____

_____.

I agree that _____

_____.

3   routine   rules   secrets

As I see it, _____

_____.

As I will clearly show, _____

_____.

I'm sure you'll agree with me when I say that _____

_____.

There is no doubt in my mind that _____

_____.

4   honesty   freedom   change

I disagree that _____

_____.

I feel certain that _____

_____.

I don't agree with the idea that _____

_____.

It seems to me that _____

_____.

Set 4: Introducing the Topic

Imagine that you think the winter break is not long enough. You want to write a letter to the school principal giving your opinion. Here is a simple introduction to the letter.

> Last winter break, we had two weeks off school. This is not a long enough break. I think you should consider making the winter break four weeks.

This introduction tells what the topic is and states the main opinion. However, there are stronger ways to introduce the topic. A better introduction will set the scene, give more details, give important background information, or help show what the problem is. Here is an example of a strong introduction.

> The winter break is an important time in the school year. It is halfway through the year and students are needing a chance to relax. It is also just a month or two before students start preparing for important assessments. The current break of just two weeks is not long enough for students to relax and recharge. I believe the winter break should be changed so that it is four weeks long.

This introduction gives more details about the topic. It sets the scene so the principal understands what the topic is and starts to see what the problem is. After introducing the topic, it then states the main idea of the letter.

In this set of writing prompts, focus on writing strong introductions. As you write an introduction, use these questions to guide you.

- Will the reader know what I am talking about?
- Is it clear exactly what the topic is?
- Have I set the scene for the reader?
- Is any necessary background information included?
- Is the main idea or opinion clearly stated?

Writing Prompt 16

You have just read an article describing how young people playing contact sports should wear mouth guards. The article described how teeth can be damaged or knocked out, and how painful and costly injuries can easily be prevented. Write an opinion piece that will persuade people playing contact sports to wear mouth guards.

Be sure to include a strong introduction that tells what the topic is and states your opinion.

Use the table below to plan your work. Then write or type your opinion piece.

Introduction: Introduce the topic and state the main opinion.   → **Write a few sentences that tell what the topic is and state the main idea.**
Supporting Ideas: Describe the reasons you will use to support the opinion.   → **Write one paragraph focused on each supporting idea.**
Conclusion: Restate the main opinion and finish off the opinion piece.   →**Write a paragraph that concludes your opinion piece.**

Writing Prompt 17

There are many websites today where you can leave reviews. Imagine you have just read a book you disliked a lot. Should you leave a bad review or would that be unfair to the author? Write an opinion piece that tells whether or not you feel that people should leave bad reviews.

Be sure to include a strong introduction that tells what the topic is and states your opinion. You can use the experience described of disliking a book to introduce the topic and set the scene.

Use the table below to plan your work. Then write or type your opinion piece.

Introduction: Introduce the topic and state the main opinion.   → Write a few sentences that tell what the topic is and state the main idea.
Supporting Ideas: Describe the reasons you will use to support the opinion.   → Write one paragraph focused on each supporting idea.
Conclusion: Restate the main opinion and finish off the opinion piece.   →Write a paragraph that concludes your opinion piece.

Writing Prompt 18

Your teacher has a plan to get a class pet that students will take turns looking after. Do you think this is a good idea? Write an opinion piece that argues that the plan to get a class pet either should or should not go ahead.

Be sure to include a strong introduction that tells what the topic is and states your opinion. Make sure you refer to the plan to get a class pet. This is necessary background information readers will need to understand your opinion.

Use the table below to plan your work. Then write or type your opinion piece.

Introduction: Introduce the topic and state the main opinion.   → Write a few sentences that tell what the topic is and state the main idea.
Supporting Ideas: Describe the reasons you will use to support the opinion.   → Write one paragraph focused on each supporting idea.
Conclusion: Restate the main opinion and finish off the opinion piece.   →Write a paragraph that concludes your opinion piece.

Writing Prompt 19

A common piece of advice people state is that you should never be afraid to speak your mind. However, sometimes it is better not to tell people how you really feel about something. Write an opinion piece that argues that sometimes it is better to keep your thoughts to yourself than to share them.

Be sure to include a strong introduction that tells what the topic is and states your opinion.

Use the table below to plan your work. Then write or type your opinion piece.

Introduction: Introduce the topic and state the main opinion.   → Write a few sentences that tell what the topic is and state the main idea.
Supporting Ideas: Describe the reasons you will use to support the opinion.   → Write one paragraph focused on each supporting idea.
Conclusion: Restate the main opinion and finish off the opinion piece.   →Write a paragraph that concludes your opinion piece.

Writing Prompt 20

Young people sometimes really want to fit in. Do you believe it is important to fit in or is it okay to be different? Write an opinion piece that tells whether you believe it is okay to be different.

Be sure to include a strong introduction that tells what the topic is and states your opinion.

Use the table below to plan your work. Then write or type your opinion piece.

Introduction: Introduce the topic and state the main opinion.   → Write a few sentences that tell what the topic is and state the main idea.
Supporting Ideas: Describe the reasons you will use to support the opinion.   → Write one paragraph focused on each supporting idea.
Conclusion: Restate the main opinion and finish off the opinion piece.   →Write a paragraph that concludes your opinion piece.

Warm-Up Exercise: Choosing a Title

The title of an opinion piece is one way to catch the attention of your readers and make them want to read it. A simple title might just state the main idea. Here are some ways you can create a better title:

- ask readers a question
- tell readers what to do
- say something interesting or catchy
- use humor
- use strong language to make the topic seem serious and important

The simple titles below are titles of opinion pieces from a school newspaper. Practice writing titles by writing three new titles for each simple title below. Focus on writing a title that will catch the reader's attention. The first one has been completed for you.

1 Simple   *We are Given Too Much Homework*

   Better   *Are You Drowning in Homework?*

   Better   *It's Home Time! No! It's Homework Time*

   Better   *Stop! We Can't Handle this Much Homework*

2 Simple   *School Dances are Always the Same*

   Better   _____

   Better   _____

   Better   _____

3 Simple *Stop Hating Mondays! Learn to Love Them!*

   Better _____

   Better _____

   Better _____

4 Simple *Try Out for the School Choir*

   Better _____

   Better _____

   Better _____

5 Simple *The Bus Waiting Areas Need More Shelter*

   Better _____

   Better _____

   Better _____

6 Simple *The Voting Age Should be Lowered*

   Better _____

   Better _____

   Better _____

Set 5: Starting Strong

You've learned that an opinion piece starts with an introduction that tells what the topic is and states the main idea. Now let's look at some ways to make the introduction strong.

A strong introduction will get readers interested in the topic and make them want to keep reading. It will make the reader care about what you are writing about. There are many different ways to do this. The table below lists some of the ways you can make the introduction strong.

Technique	Details
Use questions	Ask the reader one or more questions. This helps the reader think about the topic and relate to it.
Speak to the reader	Write as if you are talking to just one reader. You can address the reader as "you."
Use emotions	Try to make the reader feel something. You might make the reader feel excited, worried, or angry.
Set the scene	Describe a situation or event related to your topic.
Show the importance	Focus on explaining why the topic or your opinion is important.
Use facts	Start with an interesting or important fact that will catch the reader's attention.
Describe a personal experience.	Describe an event or experience from your own life that shows what the topic is.
Ask for action	Tell the reader to do something or state that something must be done.
Use a quote or proverb	Include a quote from someone famous or a proverb related to your topic.
Include humor	Use a funny story, description, or statement to both entertain and interest the reader.

The technique to use for each opinion piece will depend on what you are writing about, what type of piece you are writing, and who the audience is. Now complete the exercises to practice using the different techniques.

Writing Prompt 21

Example of the Technique: Use Questions

Fashion is always changing. Every season there is a new trend to follow or a new item or brand that everyone wants. Even if you do manage to keep up with this season, you just have to start all over again next season. Will you ever be able to keep up? How much money is wasted trying to keep up? Isn't it time to just give up on trying to keep up? Everyone should ignore fashion trends and just wear whatever they like to wear.

Write an introduction for an opinion piece with the main idea given.

Main Idea: It's better to walk away from an argument than to lose your cool.

Start by listing some questions you could ask to interest the reader in the topic.

1. _____

2. _____

3. _____

4. _____

Now write an introduction using one or more of the questions you wrote.

_____

_____

_____

_____

_____

Writing Prompt 22

Example of the Technique: Speak to the Reader

Have you ever been told a piece of gossip? Have you ever passed on a piece of gossip to someone else? Maybe you didn't think that you were gossiping. You might have just thought of it as chatting. But if you were talking about something you heard about someone, you were gossiping. While gossip can seem harmless, it can be very hurtful to the person being talked about. The school would be a much better place if people stopped gossiping.

Write an introduction for an opinion piece with the main idea below.

Main Idea: If you tell lies, you will lose people's trust.

You want the reader to relate to your topic and think about how it impacts them. Start by writing a brief summary of what you want readers to think about. (For example, "I want students to think about whether they have gossiped before.")

_____

_____

Now write an introduction that speaks to the reader.

_____

_____

_____

_____

_____

Writing Prompt 23

Example of the Technique: Use Emotions

Jess lost her eyesight when she was a young girl. For a long time, this stopped her from doing many things. Everything changed when Jess was given her guide dog Ralph. Ralph changed her life and allowed her to experience so much more of the world. Thanks to Ralph, Jess never feels like she is missing out. While many people think of dogs as pets, they can be much more than that. Dogs have many important uses in society.

Write an introduction for an opinion piece with the main idea below.

Main Idea: Teachers should not treat some students like favorites.

Start by thinking about what emotion you want people to feel and why. It could be a negative emotion like sadness, fear, or anger. It could be a positive emotion like excitement, pride, or hope. Start by writing a brief summary of what emotion you want people to feel and why. (For example, "I want people to feel hope when they learn what a guide dog can do for its owner.")

_____

_____

Now write an introduction that uses the emotion you described.

_____

_____

_____

_____

Writing Prompt 24

Example of the Technique: Set the Scene

It has been a tough day at school for Hannah. Math class was confusing, she had an argument with a friend, and she was given a low mark on her book report. Hannah is home now and goes straight to her room. She pulls the diary from her drawer and begins to write. She writes about everything that happened and how she feels. By the end of it, she is feeling much calmer. That is one of the main benefits of keeping a diary. A diary is a great way to deal with daily stresses.

Write an introduction for an opinion piece with the main idea below.

Main Idea: It's rude to play loud music at night.

Start by thinking about what scene related to the topic you want to describe. Write a brief statement about the scene you will describe and your purpose for describing the scene. (For example, "I will describe a student coping with the day's stresses to show how a diary can help.")

_____

_____

Now write an introduction that uses the scene you described.

_____

_____

_____

_____

Writing Prompt 25

Example of the Technique: Show the Importance

Many young people today listen to music on their phones. They put headphones on and enjoy escaping into the music. The problem is that these actions can cause hearing problems and hearing loss. Imagine starting to losing your hearing at just 20 years old and having to live with this forever. Luckily, if you take action now and listen to music safely, you can easily avoid these problems.

Write an introduction for an opinion piece with the main idea below.

Main Idea: It's important to wear sunscreen when spending time outdoors.

Start by thinking about how you can show the importance of your main idea. Write a brief summary of what you will describe to show the importance of your main idea. (For example, "I will describe how people can damage their hearing at a young age and have this problem for life.")

_____

_____

Now write an introduction that shows the importance of your main idea.

_____

_____

_____

_____

Writing Prompt 26

Example of the Technique: Use Facts

Arnold Schwarzenegger has led an impressive life full of achievements. He became a champion bodybuilder, winning the Mr. Olympia title seven times. He then became a Hollywood movie star. In 2003, he became Governor of California and stayed in that role until 2011. Schwarzenegger's success in all these fields is due to his determination.

Write an introduction for an opinion piece with the main idea below.

Main Idea: Steven Spielberg is one of the world's most successful directors.

Look up some facts about Spielberg's success such as awards he has won, records he has broken, or other achievements. List two facts you want to use.

1. _____

_____

2. _____

_____

Now write an introduction that includes the two facts listed above.

_____

_____

_____

_____

_____

Writing Prompt 27

Example of the Technique: Describe a Personal Experience

Rachel and I had been friends for years, but then we had a disagreement over a school project. She wouldn't listen to me and I wouldn't listen to her. We both became more and more annoyed until we stopped speaking to each other at all. The cause of the argument was not even that important. The problem was that we stopped listening to each other and both focused on being right. The need to be right is a major cause of many arguments.

Write an introduction for an opinion piece with the main idea below.

Main Idea: Laughter is one of the easiest ways to break a bad mood.

Start by thinking of a personal experience you can describe that will introduce the topic. Write a brief summary of the personal experience you are going to use. (For example, "I will describe the time a small disagreement became a major argument because Rachel and I both wanted to be right.")

_____

_____

Now write an introduction that uses the personal experience you described.

_____

_____

_____

_____

Writing Prompt 28

Example of the Technique: Ask for Action

There are many companies that still produce their goods in America. These companies have plants and factories that employ many people. They are important to the communities they are part of, and good for the country as a whole. To keep these efforts going, these companies need everyone's support. The next time you go shopping, pay attention to where goods are made and choose items that are made in America.

Write an introduction for an opinion piece with the main idea below.

Main Idea: Students should stop damaging books they borrow from the library.

Start by thinking about who you are speaking to and what action you want them to take. Write a brief summary of your audience and what you want the audience to do. (For example, "I am asking shoppers to choose products that are made in America.")

_____

_____

Now write an introduction that asks the audience you identified to take action.

_____

_____

_____

_____

Writing Prompt 29

Example of the Technique: Use a Quote or Proverb

Abraham Lincoln once said: "Give me six hours to chop down a tree and I will spend the first four sharpening the axe." Abraham Lincoln understood the importance of preparation. It is often easy to feel like you are in a hurry and that preparing is just wasting time. However, a little time preparing can save you a lot of time later. When you are set a task, always take the time to create a plan and prepare before you take any action.

Write an introduction for an opinion piece with the main idea below.

Main Idea: Nobody is perfect, so it is important to learn to forgive others.

Start by finding a quote from a well-known person or a proverb that relates to the main idea. Write the quote or proverb you are going to use below. If it is a quote, be sure to include details of who said it below and in your introduction.

_____

_____

_____

Now write an introduction that uses the quote or proverb you listed.

_____

_____

_____

_____

_____

Writing Prompt 30

Example of the Technique: Include Humor

My brother pushed the Monopoly board off the table. Little houses and hotels and fake money flew everywhere. Then he stood up and stormed away. We all laughed at him for getting so upset over a silly game. The truth is that nobody likes a bad sport. It is important to learn to lose without being silly about it.

Write an introduction for an opinion piece with the main idea below.

Main Idea: Being too curious can be a problem.

Start by thinking of a humorous scene you could describe to introduce the topic. Write a brief summary of the scene and describe your purpose for including it. (For example, "I will describe the time my brother got mad when playing Monopoly to give an example of someone being a bad sport.")

_____

_____

_____

Now write an introduction that includes a description of the humorous scene.

_____

_____

_____

_____

_____

Warm-Up Exercise: Using Concrete Details

In the next set, you will learn about using details to support opinions. The details you use are most effective when they are concrete. This means they are specific details that describe something the reader can imagine.

Here is an example of a vague detail and three concrete details.

Vague	The kitchen was very messy.
Concrete	There were dishes piled up in the sink.
Concrete	There were drops of cake batter on the floor.
Concrete	There was flour, sugar, and cocoa all over the bench.

These concrete details help the reader imagine the messy kitchen.

Practice using concrete details by listing three concrete details to replace each vague detail listed.

Vague	The school buses are very dirty.
Concrete	_____
	_____
Concrete	_____
	_____
Concrete	_____
	_____

Vague   I felt very nervous while waiting for the plane.

 Think about things you might be doing because you are nervous, such as pacing back and forth.

Concrete _____

_____

Concrete _____

_____

Concrete _____

_____

Vague   The apple pie we ordered was delicious.

Concrete _____

_____

Concrete _____

_____

Concrete _____

_____

Set 6: Using Details to Support an Opinion

Writing Prompt 31

Strong opinion pieces include good reasons to support the opinion. One way to support an opinion is to include details.

The plan below is for an opinion piece arguing that the school needs to purchase new computers. Notice that the plan includes specific details that tell exactly what is wrong with the computers. These details help the reader understand what the problem is and why it needs to be solved.

Use the plan below to write an opinion piece.

Introduction: Introduce the topic and state the main opinion.
The school computers are essential tools. The old computers are not good enough. The school needs to buy new ones.
→ **Write a few sentences that tell what the topic is and state the main idea.**
Supporting Ideas: Describe the reasons you will use to support the opinion.
The computers are slow. It takes a long time to do everything and that is annoying.
The computers often break down. Sometimes 10 of the 30 computers in the room will be out of order, so there are not enough for everyone.
The computers sometimes stop working while you are writing an essay or report. You lose the work you have done.
→ **Write one paragraph focused on each reason. Use details to help make each reason clear.**
Conclusion: Restate the main opinion and finish off the opinion piece.
Students use the school computers to learn, to do research, to complete assignments, and to take tests. Students need new computers that always work and that work well.
→**Write a paragraph that concludes your opinion piece.**

Writing Prompt 32

You believe that the schoolyard should be cleaner. Write an opinion piece arguing that the schoolyard should be cleaner. Be sure to include details that describe exactly what is wrong with the schoolyard.

Use the table below to plan your work. Then write or type your opinion piece.

Introduction: Introduce the topic and state the main opinion.
→ Write a few sentences that tell what the topic is and state the main idea.
Supporting Ideas: Describe the reasons you will use to support the opinion.
→ Write one paragraph focused on each reason. Use details to help make each reason clear.
Conclusion: Restate the main opinion and finish off the opinion piece.
→Write a paragraph that concludes your opinion piece.

Writing Prompt 33

Today, many people send e-mails instead of sending written letters. Write an opinion piece arguing that e-mails are better than written letters. Use details to explain why e-mails are better than written letters.

Use the table below to plan your work. Then write or type your opinion piece.

Introduction: Introduce the topic and state the main opinion.   → **Write a few sentences that tell what the topic is and state the main idea.**
Supporting Ideas: Describe the reasons you will use to support the opinion.   → **Write one paragraph focused on each reason. Use details to help make each reason clear.**
Conclusion: Restate the main opinion and finish off the opinion piece.   →**Write a paragraph that concludes your opinion piece.**

Writing Prompt 34

You have just read that people sometimes get injured by not being careful enough when going outside in stormy weather. You want people to be careful during stormy weather. Write an opinion piece that warns people to be careful when going outside during stormy weather. Use details to clearly describe how people can get injured and what people need to do to avoid injury.

Use the table below to plan your work. Then write or type your opinion piece.

Introduction: Introduce the topic and state the main opinion.   → Write a few sentences that tell what the topic is and state the main idea.
Supporting Ideas: Describe the reasons you will use to support the opinion.   → Write one paragraph focused on each reason. Use details to help make each reason clear.
Conclusion: Restate the main opinion and finish off the opinion piece.   →Write a paragraph that concludes your opinion piece.

Writing Prompt 35

Think of a change that your teacher could make so that learning is more fun. Write an opinion piece arguing that the change should be made. Be sure to include details to show why the change should be made and how the change would make learning more fun.

Use the table below to plan your work. Then write or type your opinion piece.

Introduction: Introduce the topic and state the main opinion.   → Write a few sentences that tell what the topic is and state the main idea.
Supporting Ideas: Describe the reasons you will use to support the opinion.   → Write one paragraph focused on each reason. Use details to help make each reason clear.
Conclusion: Restate the main opinion and finish off the opinion piece.   →Write a paragraph that concludes your opinion piece.

Warm-Up Exercise: Choosing a Topic

Sometimes writing prompts will ask your opinion on a general idea. For example, you might be asked whether or not it is important to be cautious. When deciding on supporting ideas and examples, it is a good idea to keep your work focused on one topic. Here are three different topics that could be used in an essay about being cautious.

- Being cautious when making decisions
- Being cautious when taking part in sports and activities
- Being cautious when you are on the Internet

A strong opinion piece will choose one of these topics and use supporting ideas and examples related to that topic. This will stop the opinion piece from being too broad and make sure it doesn't jump between too many different ideas.

A good way to start planning opinion pieces with general ideas is to first list a few different specific topics you could use. Then you can decide which topic to focus on in your work. Each exercise below gives a writing prompt with a general idea. List a few specific topics you could use for each general idea given.

1 Idea   Creativity is a great quality to have.

Topic 1   _____

_____

Topic 2   _____

_____

Topic 3   _____

_____

2 Idea   It is important to be understanding toward others.

Topic 1 _____

_____

Topic 2 _____

_____

Topic 3 _____

_____

Topic 4 _____

_____

3 Idea   It is important not to be selfish.

Topic 1 _____

_____

Topic 2 _____

_____

Topic 3 _____

_____

Topic 4 _____

_____

Set 7: Using Examples to Support an Opinion

Writing Prompt 36

Think of someone you know who you think is kind. Write an opinion piece supporting the idea that the person is kind.

To write this opinion piece, you'll need to include examples of how the person is kind. Think of three specific examples of times when the person was kind.

Use the table below to plan your work. Be sure to include three examples that show that the person is kind. Then write or type your opinion piece.

Introduction: Introduce the topic and state the main opinion.   → Write a few sentences that tell what the topic is and state the main idea.
Supporting Ideas: Describe the examples you will use to support the opinion.   → Write one paragraph focused on each example.
Conclusion: Restate the main opinion and finish off the opinion piece.   →Write a paragraph that concludes your opinion piece.

Writing Prompt 37

Write an opinion piece that supports the statement below.

   Spending time outdoors is good for you.

Use the table below to plan your work. Be sure to include three examples to support the opinion. Then write or type your opinion piece.

Introduction: Introduce the topic and state the main opinion.   → Write a few sentences that tell what the topic is and state the main idea.
Supporting Ideas: Describe the examples you will use to support the opinion.   → Write one paragraph focused on each example.
Conclusion: Restate the main opinion and finish off the opinion piece.   →Write a paragraph that concludes your opinion piece.

Writing Prompt 38

Write an opinion piece that supports the statement below.

Having a good sense of humor makes life easier.

Use the table below to plan your work. Be sure to include three examples to support the opinion. Then write or type your opinion piece.

Introduction: Introduce the topic and state the main opinion.
→ Write a few sentences that tell what the topic is and state the main idea.
Supporting Ideas: Describe the examples you will use to support the opinion.
→ Write one paragraph focused on each example.
Conclusion: Restate the main opinion and finish off the opinion piece.
→Write a paragraph that concludes your opinion piece.

Writing Prompt 39

Write an opinion piece that supports the statement below.

    You can learn a lot from people who are older than you.

Use the table below to plan your work. Be sure to include three examples to support the opinion. Then write or type your opinion piece.

Introduction: Introduce the topic and state the main opinion.   → Write a few sentences that tell what the topic is and state the main idea.
Supporting Ideas: Describe the examples you will use to support the opinion.   → Write one paragraph focused on each example.
Conclusion: Restate the main opinion and finish off the opinion piece.   →Write a paragraph that concludes your opinion piece.

Writing Prompt 40

Write an opinion piece that supports the statement below.

It is annoying when people are too bossy.

Use the table below to plan your work. Be sure to include three examples to support the opinion. Then write or type your opinion piece.

Introduction: Introduce the topic and state the main opinion.   → Write a few sentences that tell what the topic is and state the main idea.
Supporting Ideas: Describe the examples you will use to support the opinion.   → Write one paragraph focused on each example.
Conclusion: Restate the main opinion and finish off the opinion piece.   →Write a paragraph that concludes your opinion piece.

Warm-Up Exercise: Personal Experiences and Meaning

In the next set, you will learn how to use personal experiences to support an opinion. The diagram below summarizes a personal experience a student used in an essay. The experience was described to support the opinion that you should always be willing to try new things.

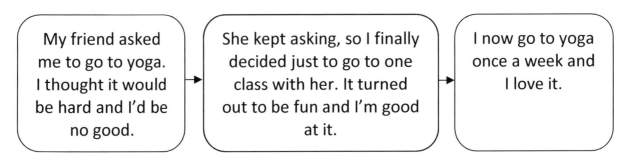

Now practice thinking of personal experiences that can be used in opinion pieces. For each main idea given, briefly describe two situations from your own life that could be used to support the main idea.

1   Main Idea: It is important to ask for help when you need it.

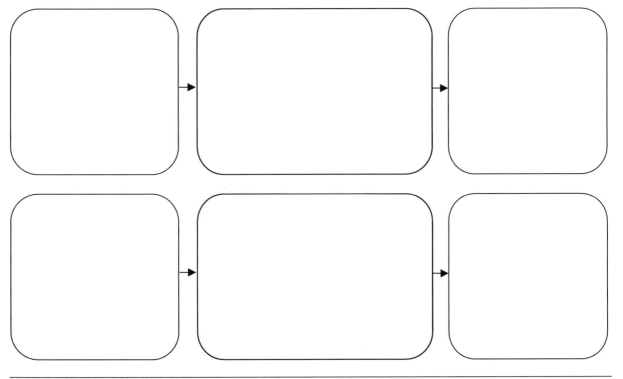

2 Main Idea: Things are not always as bad as they seem.

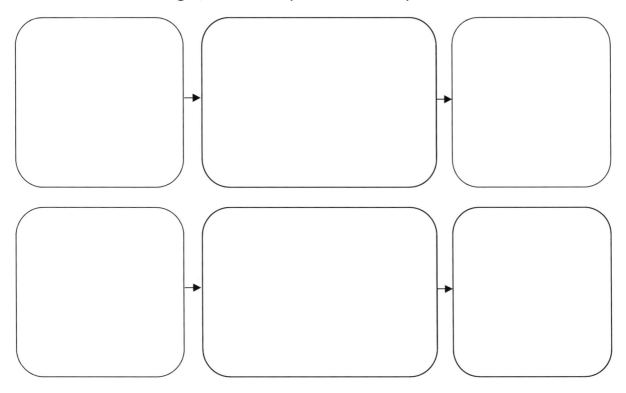

3 Main Idea: Surprises can bring people great joy.

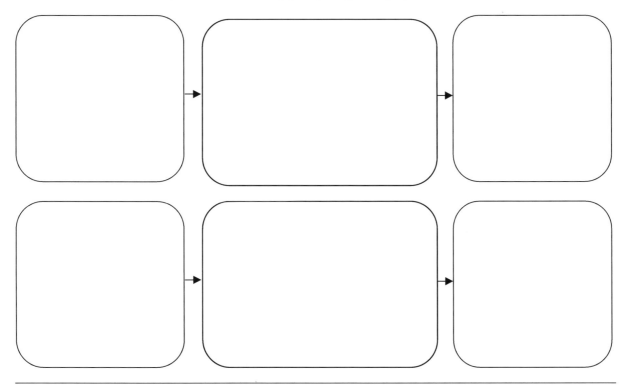

Set 8: Using Personal Experience to Support an Opinion

Writing Prompt 41

Read the writing prompt below.

> Even great friends fight sometimes. Having an argument with a friend does not mean the friendship is over.

A good way to support this opinion piece would be to describe a situation from your own life that shows that the statement is true. You could describe a time when you argued with someone but still remained friends. You could also describe two people you know who argued but later made up.

Now think of a real personal experience you could use in an opinion piece with that topic. Describe the personal experience below.

_____

_____

_____

_____

_____

_____

_____

Writing Prompt 42

Read the writing prompt below.

> Be careful who you tell your secrets to. Some people cannot be trusted with secrets.

Think of some situations from your own life you could use to support the statement. You could describe how you shared a secret you shouldn't have or how someone shared a secret you trusted them with. List three ideas below.

☐ _____

☐ _____

☐ _____

Select the situation you think would best support the statement. Describe the situation below and explain how it supports the opinion.

_____
_____
_____
_____
_____
_____

Writing Prompt 43

Read the writing prompt below.

    Sometimes breaking the rules is the right thing to do.

Think of some personal experiences you could use to support the statement. You might describe times when you or someone you know broke a rule, or a time when you should have broken a rule. List three ideas below.

☐ _____

☐ _____

☐ _____

Select the personal experience you think would best support the statement. Describe the personal experience below and explain how it supports the opinion.

_____
_____
_____
_____
_____
_____
_____

Writing Prompt 44

Read the writing prompt below.

> It is important to learn from your mistakes so you do not repeat them.

Think of some personal experiences you could use to support the statement. You might describe a time you learned from a mistake or a time you kept repeating the same mistake because you didn't learn from it. List three ideas below.

- ☐ _____

- ☐ _____

- ☐ _____

Select the personal experience you think would best support the statement. Describe the personal experience below and explain how it supports the opinion.

_____

_____

_____

_____

_____

_____

_____

Writing Prompt 45

Sometimes the first impression you have of someone is incorrect. Think of a time when your first impression of someone was wrong. Use a description of that time to show that it is important not to judge people based on first impressions.

Use the table below to plan your work. Then write or type your opinion piece.

Introduction: Introduce the topic and state the main opinion.
→ **Write a few sentences that tell what the topic is and state the main idea.**
Supporting Ideas: Describe the personal experience that supports the main idea. Tell what your first impression was, why it was wrong, and what you learned from the experience.
→ **Write two or three paragraphs describing your experience.**
Conclusion: Restate the main opinion and finish off the opinion piece.
→**Write a paragraph that concludes your opinion piece.**

Warm-Up Exercise: Using Linking Words and Phrases

Linking words and phrases are used to connect ideas. They can be used to show how a reason supports an idea or to show cause and effect between ideas.

In each example below, the linking word or phrase is underlined. Complete each sentence in a way that makes sense.

1 Most jobs require good computer skills, <u>so</u> _____

_____.

2 There are only 40 bike racks, but over one hundred students ride to school.

<u>Therefore</u>, _____.

3 The basketball team train the hardest and have the best coach. <u>Consequently</u>,

_____.

4 <u>As a result</u> of the high cost of going to the camp, _____

_____.

5 There is more graffiti appearing at the school. <u>In order to</u> stop this, _____

_____.

6 Not all dogs that appear friendly really are. <u>For this reason</u>, _____

_____.

Set 9: Using Facts to Support an Opinion

Writing Prompt 46

Read the main idea of an opinion piece below.

    Bees are very important insects.

An opinion piece on this topic would use facts about bees to show what makes them important. Use the Internet or books to find some facts about bees that support the main idea. List three facts below.

1. _____

2. _____

3. _____

Use the facts you found to write a paragraph with the main idea above.

_____
_____
_____
_____

Writing Prompt 47

Read the main idea of an opinion piece below.

> Carving the Mount Rushmore National Memorial was a great achievement.

Use the Internet or books to find some facts that support the main idea. List three facts below.

1. _____

   _____

2. _____

   _____

3. _____

   _____

Use the facts you found to write a paragraph with the main idea above.

_____

_____

_____

_____

_____

Writing Prompt 48

Read the main idea of an opinion piece below.

Niagara Falls shows how amazing nature can be.

Use the Internet or books to find some facts that support the main idea. List three facts below.

1. _____

_____

2. _____

_____

3. _____

_____

Use the facts you found to write a paragraph with the main idea above.

_____

_____

_____

_____

_____

_____

Writing Prompt 49

Read the main idea of an opinion piece below.

Albert Einstein was one of the most important scientists in history.

Use the Internet or books to find some facts that support the main idea. List three facts below.

1. _____
   _____

2. _____
   _____

3. _____
   _____

Use the facts you found to write a paragraph with the main idea above.

_____
_____
_____
_____
_____
_____

Writing Prompt 50

Read the main idea of an opinion piece below.

    It is important to drink enough water each day.

Use the Internet or books to find some facts that support the main idea. List three facts below.

1. _____

   _____

2. _____

   _____

3. _____

   _____

Use the facts you found to write a paragraph with the main idea above.

_____

_____

_____

_____

_____

_____

Warm-Up Exercise: Introducing the Conclusion

Conclusions often start with a sentence restating the main idea. However, the main idea should not be worded exactly the same as in the introduction. Instead, it should be restated using different wording. For each main idea below, write a sentence that restates the main idea in a different way. The first one has been completed for you.

1 There is no need to be afraid of change.

   <u>As you can see, change is not something that needs to be feared.</u>

2 It is better to remain calm than to become angry.

   _____

3 People need to stop wasting so much water.

   _____

4 Everyone should be prepared for winter storms.

   _____

5 Movies today are not as funny as they used to be.

   _____

6 Exercise shouldn't feel like a chore.

   _____

Set 10: Writing the Conclusion

Writing Prompt 51

The last paragraph of an opinion piece is the conclusion. The conclusion should restate the main idea. However, it shouldn't use exactly the same words as the introduction. Instead, it should say the same thing in a different way. It may also restate the reasons or supporting ideas. Finally, it should finish in a way that ends the whole opinion piece neatly.

Now read the overview of an opinion piece a student wrote.

Main Idea: Going fishing can be a very boring experience.

Supporting Idea 1: You often have to wait a long time for bites.

Supporting Idea 2: There is nothing you can do except sit and wait.

Supporting Idea 3: Even after hours, you still might not catch a fish.

Write a paragraph that could be used to conclude the opinion piece.

_____

_____

_____

_____

_____

_____

Writing Prompt 52

Haley wrote an essay arguing that keeping up with computer technology is hard.

Read the overview of the opinion piece below.

Main Idea: It is difficult to keep up with changes in computer technology.

Supporting Idea 1: There are always new and better computers being released.

Supporting Idea 2: Replacing a computer every few months costs too much.

Supporting Idea 3: Replacing computers often creates a lot of waste.

Write a paragraph that could be used to conclude the opinion piece.

_____

_____

_____

_____

_____

_____

_____

Writing Prompt 53

Maxine wrote an essay arguing that everyone should learn to grow food.

Read the overview of the opinion piece below.

Main Idea: Growing your own fruit and vegetables is a useful hobby.

Supporting Idea 1: The food you grow yourself is fresher.

Supporting Idea 2: Fresh food from your garden tastes better.

Supporting Idea 3: It can save you money.

Write a paragraph that could be used to conclude the opinion piece.

_____

_____

_____

_____

_____

_____

_____

Writing Prompt 54

Owen wrote a letter arguing that the cafeteria should be cleaner.

Read the overview of the opinion piece below.

Main Idea: The school cafeteria needs to be kept cleaner.

Supporting Idea 1: It is not healthy to eat in a place that is not clean.

Supporting Idea 2: A dirty cafeteria attracts bugs.

Supporting Idea 3: It is not a place students enjoy spending time.

Write a paragraph that could be used to conclude the opinion piece.

_____

_____

_____

_____

_____

_____

_____

Writing Prompt 55

Austin wrote a letter asking that people attend the science fair.

Read the overview of the opinion piece below.

Main Idea: Please come along to the science fair on Friday.

Supporting Idea 1: There are many great displays to see.

Supporting Idea 2: You will learn lots of interesting things.

Supporting Idea 3: Students have worked hard and deserve your support.

Write a paragraph that could be used to conclude the opinion piece.

_____

_____

_____

_____

_____

_____

_____

_____

Warm-Up Exercise: Using Strong Language

You can use strong language to help make your points clearer in opinion pieces and to have a greater impact on the reader. Read the sentences below.

I <u>think that</u> everyone needs a good friend during <u>hard</u> times.
I <u>firmly believe that</u> everyone needs a good friend during <u>tough</u> times.

The second sentence is more effective because it uses stronger language. Now practice using strong words by replacing the underlined words in each sentence with stronger ones.

1 Staying up too late will make you feel <u>tired</u> the next day.

   Staying up too late will make you feel _____ the next day.

2 I <u>feel that</u> all students would like a <u>better</u> menu.

   I _____ all students would like a _____ menu.

3 It is <u>not right</u> that the choir has to pay for their own travel.

   It is _____ that the choir has to pay for their own travel.

4 Tickets to the school play this year are <u>too costly</u>.

   Tickets to the school play this year are _____.

5 I <u>ask</u> all readers to <u>think about</u> adopting a cat.

   I _____ all readers to _____ adopting a cat.

Set 11: Using Calls to Action

Writing Prompt 56

The purpose of an opinion piece is to get the reader to agree with your opinion or to do something. The introduction and body have shown what your opinion is and why the reader should agree. Many opinion pieces can be ended well by using a call to action. This is a statement that asks the reader to agree with you or to take some sort of action.

Here is an example of a conclusion that ends with a call to action. The call to action is underlined. It first tells the reader that action must be taken. It then describes the action to be taken. It ends with a sentence describing the result of taking action.

> It is now clear that there are not enough buses running. They are too crowded and one bus an hour simply isn't enough. There is too much waiting and it isn't convenient enough. <u>This change has been delayed for far too long and action must be taken now. It's time to create a new schedule where buses run every half hour. This will be more convenient for everyone and people will use the buses more.</u>

Now practice writing calls to action by writing another example of a call to action to end the paragraph.

It is now clear that there are not enough buses running. They are too crowded and one bus an hour simply isn't enough. There is too much waiting and it isn't convenient enough.

_____

_____

_____

_____

Writing Prompt 57

Jasmine wrote an essay arguing that people should support local businesses. The first few sentences of the conclusion are given below.

Practice writing calls to action by finishing the conclusion below with a call to action. Your call to action should encourage people to shop at local businesses.

Start by making some notes on what action you want readers to take, why action should be taken, or what the result will be of taking action.

Notes

Use your notes to write an ending to the conclusion that includes a call to action.

Conclusion

As I have described, local businesses are an important part of the community. They are of great benefit to everyone. If we want them to survive, we need to support them.

_____

_____

_____

_____

_____

Writing Prompt 58

Tai wrote an essay arguing that people should not text while driving. The first few sentences of the conclusion are given below.

Practice writing calls to action by finishing the conclusion below with a call to action. Your call to action should urge people not to text while driving.

Start by making some notes on what action you want readers to take, why action should be taken, or what the result will be of taking action.

Notes

Use your notes to write an ending to the conclusion that includes a call to action.

Conclusion

Texting while driving is very dangerous. The driver is not watching the road at all times and is not concentrating. There is no excuse for this dangerous behavior.

_____

_____

_____

_____

Writing Prompt 59

Yuri wrote a letter encouraging students to sign up for the school play. The first few sentences of the conclusion are given below.

Practice writing calls to action by finishing the conclusion below with a call to action. Your call to action should encourage students to sign up for the play.

Start by making some notes on what action you want readers to take, why action should be taken, or what the result will be of taking action.

Notes

Use your notes to write an ending to the conclusion that includes a call to action.

Conclusion

The school play could not be a success without the help of a huge team of students. Students are needed to perform in the play, as well as complete other tasks like managing lighting, creating costumes, and designing sets.

_____

_____

_____

_____

_____

Writing Prompt 60

Jamison wrote a book review asking people to read the books of Louis Sachar. The first few sentences of the conclusion are given below.

Practice writing calls to action by finishing the conclusion below with a call to action. Your call to action should encourage people to read the books.

Start by making some notes on what action you want readers to take, why action should be taken, or what the result will be of taking action.

Notes

Use your notes to write an ending to the conclusion that includes a call to action.

Conclusion

Louis Sachar is a great American children's author. His books have won many awards and are loved by children all over the world. His books are easy to read, always entertaining, and are filled with fascinating characters and storylines.

_____

_____

_____

_____

_____

Applying Writing Skills

The exercises in this section will provide practice writing different types of opinion pieces. Each set focuses on one type of writing.

Follow the instructions for each writing prompt, and plan your work in the space provided. Then write or type an opinion piece of 1 to 2 pages.

After completing your work, review your writing. You can use the checklist on the next page to help you review your work.

Review Checklist

After you finish writing your opinion piece, you can use this guide to review and edit your work. Use the questions as a guide to finding ways you can improve your work.

Writing Checklist

- ✓ Does your work have one clear opinion?
- ✓ Does your work have a strong opening? Does the opening introduce the topic and state the opinion?
- ✓ Is your opinion supported? Does your work include clear reasons and supporting ideas?
- ✓ Have you used facts, details, and examples to support your opinion?
- ✓ Is your work organized well? Is related information grouped together? Does each paragraph have one main idea?
- ✓ Is your work focused? Does all the information relate to your main ideas? Is there any information that is not needed?
- ✓ Do your ideas flow well? Have you used words and phrases to link ideas well?
- ✓ Does your work have a strong ending? Does the ending restate the main idea and tie up the opinion piece?

Editing Checklist

- ✓ Have you used a variety of sentence structures? Are your sentences all written correctly?
- ✓ Is the grammar correct?
- ✓ Are all words spelled correctly? You can check the spelling of any words you are not sure of.
- ✓ Is punctuation used correctly?
- ✓ Are all words capitalized correctly?

Set 12: Write an Opinion Essay

Writing Prompt 61

You have just read an article describing how cartoons on television are getting more violent. You believe that people under 10 shouldn't watch violent cartoons. Write an essay arguing that watching violent cartoons is bad for young children. Be sure to use two or three reasons to support your opinion.

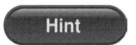

The writing prompt tells you what you need to argue. Focus on coming up with good reasons to show why young children shouldn't watch violent cartoons. Brainstorm a list of reasons below. Then choose the two or three strongest reasons and use these in your essay.

Notes and Ideas

Use the space below to make notes, brainstorm, or organize your ideas.

Planning Page

Use the table below to plan your writing. Then write or type your essay.

Introduction: Introduce the topic and state the main opinion.   → Write a few sentences that tell what the topic is and state the main idea.
Supporting Ideas: Describe the reasons you will use to support the opinion.   → Write one paragraph focused on each supporting idea.
Conclusion: Restate the main opinion and finish off the opinion piece.   →Write a paragraph that concludes your opinion piece.

Writing Prompt 62

Every four years, the Summer Olympics are held. Athletes from around the world compete to be the best in their field and receive a gold medal. It takes years of training and sacrifice to reach the Olympics. Many athletes don't make it at all, and many that do still do not win. Write an essay giving your opinion on why you think people try to achieve such a difficult goal. Include three reasons in your essay.

Remember that you will be explaining why people choose to compete in the Olympics. The writing prompt has told you the reasons against it, or the cons. You need to focus on the reasons for competing, or the pros. What do you think people gain from it? How would it feel to represent your country at the Olympics? How would it feel to win? Why would it be a good experience? The answers to these questions will help you think of the pros.

Notes and Ideas

Use the space below to make notes, brainstorm, or organize your ideas.

Planning Page

Use the table below to plan your writing. Then write or type your essay.

Introduction: Introduce the topic and state the main opinion.
→ **Write a few sentences that tell what the topic is and state the main idea.**
Supporting Ideas: Describe the reasons you will use to support the opinion.
→ **Write one paragraph focused on each supporting idea.**
Conclusion: Restate the main opinion and finish off the opinion piece.
→**Write a paragraph that concludes your opinion piece.**

Writing Prompt 63

Think about teams you have been in. What three qualities do you think are most important in a good teammate? Write an essay describing what you think makes a good teammate.

Start planning this essay by deciding on the three qualities you think are most important. Then plan to write one paragraph that explains why each quality is important. Each paragraph should include an example or a description of why the quality is important. For example, if you are going to argue that a good teammate encourages others, you could think of an example of a time when a teammate encouraged others. You could also describe the benefits of having a teammate who encourages others.

Notes and Ideas

Use the space below to make notes, brainstorm, or organize your ideas.

Planning Page

Use the table below to plan your writing. Then write or type your essay.

Introduction: Introduce the topic and state the main opinion.
→ Write a few sentences that tell what the topic is and state the main idea.
Supporting Ideas: Describe the reasons you will use to support the opinion.
→ Write one paragraph focused on each supporting idea.
Conclusion: Restate the main opinion and finish off the opinion piece.
→Write a paragraph that concludes your opinion piece.

Writing Prompt 64

Many people choose to shop online instead of shopping in stores. Do you think it is better to shop online than to shop in stores?

Write an essay telling whether or not you believe that shopping online is better than shopping in stores. Give three reasons to support your opinion.

There are benefits and drawbacks to both shopping online and shopping in stores. You could start by writing a list of pros (benefits) and cons (drawbacks) for each option. Then decide which option has more benefits than drawbacks. If you argue that shopping online is better, you can use the pros of shopping online or the cons of shopping in stores to support your opinion. If you argue that shopping in stores is better, you can use the pros of shopping in stores or the cons of shopping online to support your opinion.

Notes and Ideas

Use the space below to make notes, brainstorm, or organize your ideas.

Planning Page

Use the table below to plan your writing. Then write or type your essay.

Introduction: Introduce the topic and state the main opinion.
→ Write a few sentences that tell what the topic is and state the main idea.
Supporting Ideas: Describe the reasons you will use to support the opinion.
→ Write one paragraph focused on each supporting idea.
Conclusion: Restate the main opinion and finish off the opinion piece.
→Write a paragraph that concludes your opinion piece.

Set 13: Write a Letter

Writing Prompt 65

Your cousin Aiden has just written you a letter. He has told you how he is upset because he used to be the best baseball pitcher. However, a new student at his school is better. Aiden is upset that he does not get to pitch as much and that he does not get praised like he used to. He is so upset that he is thinking of quitting the team and wants your advice on what to do. Do you think he should quit the team? Write a letter to your cousin giving him your advice on what to do. Be sure to include two or three reasons to support your opinion.

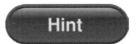

As you write this letter, remember that you are writing to a cousin. When you are writing to somebody you know well, you do not have to be formal. You can write in a more casual and chatty way.

However, your letter should still be organized well. It should have the same basic structure as an essay. The introduction should include a greeting and then state the main idea. The body should give your reasons. The conclusion will then restate the main idea and include an ending that ties everything up.

Notes and Ideas

Use the space below to make notes, brainstorm, or organize your ideas.

Planning Page

Use the table below to plan your writing. Then write or type your letter.

Introduction: Introduce the topic and state the main opinion.
→ **Write a few sentences that tell what the topic is and state the main idea.**
Supporting Ideas: Describe the reasons you will use to support the opinion.
→ **Write one paragraph focused on each supporting idea.**
Conclusion: Restate the main opinion and finish off the opinion piece.
→**Write a paragraph that concludes your opinion piece.**

Writing Prompt 66

You believe that your school needs to purchase new computers. The current computers are old, run slowly, and often break down. Write a letter to the school principal arguing that the school needs new computers. Include details and reasons to support your opinion.

This letter is to the school principal and will be more formal than the letter you wrote to your cousin. You should use more formal language. You should also sound more serious and less chatty. It is also important to remain polite while making your argument. You can do this by staying focused on the problems and why a solution is needed.

Notes and Ideas

Use the space below to make notes, brainstorm, or organize your ideas.

Planning Page

Use the table below to plan your writing. Then write or type your letter.

Introduction: Introduce the topic and state the main opinion.
→ Write a few sentences that tell what the topic is and state the main idea.
Supporting Ideas: Describe the reasons you will use to support the opinion.
→ Write one paragraph focused on each supporting idea.
Conclusion: Restate the main opinion and finish off the opinion piece.
→Write a paragraph that concludes your opinion piece.

Writing Prompt 67

Your friend Erin has written you a letter asking for your advice. Erin wants to try out for the school soccer team. However, she is worried because she will be the only girl on the team. Write a letter to Erin giving your opinion on whether or not she should try out for the team. Be sure to explain why you have that opinion.

This is a writing prompt where you could argue either way. You could try to persuade Erin that she should join the soccer team or that she should not join the soccer team. Before you start planning your letter, be sure you have decided which way you want to argue. Then stay focused on making that argument.

Notes and Ideas

Use the space below to make notes, brainstorm, or organize your ideas.

Planning Page

Use the table below to plan your writing. Then write or type your letter.

Introduction: Introduce the topic and state the main opinion.
→ **Write a few sentences that tell what the topic is and state the main idea.**
Supporting Ideas: Describe the reasons you will use to support the opinion.
→ **Write one paragraph focused on each supporting idea.**
Conclusion: Restate the main opinion and finish off the opinion piece.
→**Write a paragraph that concludes your opinion piece.**

Writing Prompt 68

You believe that students in your science class should be able to choose their own topics to study. You feel that it would be better if students could learn about what interested them instead of everyone having to learn the same thing. Write a letter to your science teacher suggesting that students be allowed to choose their own topics to study. Include three reasons to support your opinion.

Hint

When you start your letter, remember to introduce the topic before you state your main idea. Don't start simply by stating that students should be able to choose their own topics to study. Instead, introduce the topic of science class and what is studied in science class. Then finish your introduction with the main idea.

Notes and Ideas

Use the space below to make notes, brainstorm, or organize your ideas.

Planning Page

Use the table below to plan your writing. Then write or type your letter.

Introduction: Introduce the topic and state the main opinion.
→ Write a few sentences that tell what the topic is and state the main idea.
Supporting Ideas: Describe the reasons you will use to support the opinion.
→ Write one paragraph focused on each supporting idea.
Conclusion: Restate the main opinion and finish off the opinion piece.
→Write a paragraph that concludes your opinion piece.

Set 14: Write in Response to a Quote

Writing Prompt 69

Read this proverb about giving.

It is a greater gift to give than to receive.

The proverb suggests that being generous is a good thing, but it is also possible to be too generous and to give too much. Write an essay arguing that it is possible to be too generous.

This writing prompt can be supported by using examples. Think of examples of times when you or someone you know gave too much. These could be examples of giving too much money, too much of your time, or too much help. They could also be examples of times when someone took advantage of your generosity. Choose two or three strong examples and use these to support your main idea.

Notes and Ideas

Use the space below to make notes, brainstorm, or organize your ideas.

Planning Page

Use the table below to plan your writing. Then write or type your essay.

Introduction: Introduce the topic and state the main opinion.
→ Write a few sentences that tell what the topic is and state the main idea.
Supporting Ideas: Describe the examples you will use to support the opinion.
→ Write one paragraph focused on each example.
Conclusion: Restate the main opinion and finish off the opinion piece.
→Write a paragraph that concludes your opinion piece.

Writing Prompt 70

Read this proverb about facing challenges.

When the going gets tough, the tough get going.

The proverb refers to facing challenges or tough times. It describes how strong people face the tough times and take action to overcome the problems. Write an essay persuading people to be strong during tough times and to face challenges and overcome them. Use examples and details in your answer.

Hint

In this essay, you'll want to show that people can face challenges and overcome them by remaining strong and by taking action. You can do this by describing one personal experience related to this topic in detail. First, think of an example where you had a difficult problem or were in a tough situation. Then use this example throughout your essay.

In the first paragraph of the body, describe the situation and tell why it was tough. In the second paragraph, explain how you took action to overcome the problem or deal with the situation. In the final paragraph, describe how being tough allowed you to deal with the situation.

Notes and Ideas

Use the space below to make notes, brainstorm, or organize your ideas.

Planning Page

Use the table below to plan your writing. Then write or type your essay.

Introduction: Introduce the topic and state the main opinion.   → Write a few sentences that tell what the topic is and state the main idea.
Supporting Ideas: Describe the personal experience you will use to support the opinion.   → Write two or three paragraphs describing the personal experience.
Conclusion: Restate the main opinion and finish off the opinion piece.   →Write a paragraph that concludes your opinion piece.

Writing Prompt 71

Read this quote from fashion designer Roberto Cavalli.

"In the beginning, I loved being famous, but now I am tired of it and I would like to go back to my freedom."

Many people think it would be great to be famous, but there are also downsides. Write an essay arguing that being famous is not all good. Include three problems that famous people might have.

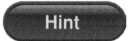

The three problems that famous people might have will be your supporting ideas. They will show that there are downsides to being famous. Read the quote again and focus on what Roberto Cavalli says. He refers to being tired and to losing his freedom. Think about why being famous might be tiring, or how being famous would cause you to lose your freedom.

Notes and Ideas

Use the space below to make notes, brainstorm, or organize your ideas.

Planning Page

Use the table below to plan your writing. Then write or type your essay.

Introduction: Introduce the topic and state the main opinion.
→ Write a few sentences that tell what the topic is and state the main idea.
Supporting Ideas: Describe the reasons you will use to support the opinion.
→ Write one paragraph focused on each supporting idea.
Conclusion: Restate the main opinion and finish off the opinion piece.
→Write a paragraph that concludes your opinion piece.

Writing Prompt 72

Read this quote from Greek playwright Aeschylus.

"There are times when fear is good. It must keep its watchful place at the heart's controls."

Write an essay arguing that fear can be a good thing. Use examples and details in your answer.

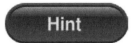

The quote from Aeschylus introduces the topic. However, you do not need to refer to Aeschylus in your essay. The purpose of the quote is simply to make you start thinking about the topic.

In your essay, focus on arguing that fear is a good thing. To do this, think of examples where fear benefits people. The topic of fear is very broad, so it is a good idea to focus on just one topic. For example, you could focus on schoolwork and use examples such as fear of failing a test making you prepare well for it. You could focus on outdoor activities and use examples such as fear of getting injured causing people to be careful. Once you choose a topic, think of three examples related to that topic to use to support your argument.

Notes and Ideas

Use the space below to make notes, brainstorm, or organize your ideas.

Planning Page

Use the table below to plan your writing. Then write or type your essay.

Introduction: Introduce the topic and state the main opinion.   → Write a few sentences that tell what the topic is and state the main idea.
Supporting Ideas: Describe the examples you will use to support the opinion.   → Write one paragraph focused on each example.
Conclusion: Restate the main opinion and finish off the opinion piece.   →Write a paragraph that concludes your opinion piece.

Set 15: Write an Article

Writing Prompt 73

Write an article for your school newspaper with the title below.

Good Manners and Cell Phone Use

Your article should give advice on how to use a cell phone without being impolite and persuade readers to follow the advice. Be sure to include three things people should do or should avoid doing when using a cell phone.

As you plan your work, think about the audience. The article is for the school newspaper, so the audience is other students. Be sure to use examples that students will relate to. The language and tone should also suit the audience.

To write this article, you will need to think of three pieces of advice. You can use your own ideas and experiences. You could also ask friends what they think people do that is rude, or use the Internet to do some research. Use one or all three of these methods to come up with three important pieces of advice.

Notes and Ideas

Use the space below to make notes, brainstorm, or organize your ideas.

Planning Page

Use the table below to plan your writing. Then write or type your article.

Introduction: Introduce the topic and state the main opinion.
→ **Write a few sentences that tell what the topic is and state the main idea.**
Supporting Ideas: Describe the three pieces of advice you will give.
→ **Write one paragraph focused on each piece of advice.**
Conclusion: Restate the main opinion and finish off the opinion piece.
→**Write a paragraph that concludes your opinion piece.**

Writing Prompt 74

Write an article for a magazine with the title below.

How to Stay Calm when Taking Tests

Your article should convince readers that it is possible to stay calm when taking tests. It should give advice or tips for staying calm, and persuade readers to follow the advice.

Before you write your article, do some research. Use books or the Internet to look up some tips or methods for reducing nervousness and staying calm. Choose the pieces of advice that you think would most help people.

In these prompts, you are being asked to write articles instead of essays. Consider using subheadings to help organize your work. For each piece of advice in the body, include a subheading that states the main idea. This will highlight your main ideas, make the advice stand out to readers, and suit the style of writing you are creating.

Notes and Ideas

Use the space below to make notes, brainstorm, or organize your ideas.

Planning Page

Use the table below to plan your writing. Then write or type your article.

Introduction: Introduce the topic and state the main opinion.
→ Write a few sentences that tell what the topic is and state the main idea.
Supporting Ideas: Describe the advice, methods, or tips you will include.
→ Write one paragraph focused on each piece of advice.
Conclusion: Restate the main opinion and finish off the opinion piece.
→Write a paragraph that concludes your opinion piece.

Writing Prompt 75

Write an article for a magazine with the title below.

Never Give Up: Three Ways to Stay Motivated and Achieve Your Goals

Your article should give advice on the topic and persuade readers to follow the advice. Be sure to include three things people should do to stay motivated.

Remember to include a strong start to your article. You want readers to be interested in the topic and to feel excited about staying motivated and achieving their goals. This will mean they'll want to read the article to find out how. You might consider asking questions, using emotions by describing the feeling of achieving a goal, or speaking to the reader.

Notes and Ideas

Use the space below to make notes, brainstorm, or organize your ideas.

Planning Page

Use the table below to plan your writing. Then write or type your article.

Introduction: Introduce the topic and state the main opinion.
→ **Write a few sentences that tell what the topic is and state the main idea.**
Supporting Ideas: Describe the three pieces of advice you will give.
→ **Write one paragraph focused on each piece of advice.**
Conclusion: Restate the main opinion and finish off the opinion piece.
→**Write a paragraph that concludes your opinion piece.**

Writing Prompt 76

Write an article for the school newspaper with the title below.

Everyone Should Learn a Second Language

Your article should persuade readers to learn a second language. Be sure to include three reasons that everyone should learn a second language.

Remember to stay focused on the purpose of your article. Your purpose is not to teach people a second language or tell people how to learn a language. These types of articles would be informational articles. Your purpose is to persuade people to want to learn a second language. Keep focused on giving reasons for learning a second language and making readers agree that learning a second language would be a good idea.

Notes and Ideas

Use the space below to make notes, brainstorm, or organize your ideas.

Planning Page

Use the table below to plan your writing. Then write or type your article.

Introduction: Introduce the topic and state the main opinion.
→ Write a few sentences that tell what the topic is and state the main idea.
Supporting Ideas: Describe the reasons you will use to support the opinion.
→ Write one paragraph focused on each supporting idea.
Conclusion: Restate the main opinion and finish off the opinion piece.
→Write a paragraph that concludes your opinion piece.

Set 16: Write a Letter to the Editor

Writing Prompt 77

Imagine that your school cafeteria offers the same simple food choices every day. You believe that the food becomes boring and that there is more variety needed. Write a letter to the editor to be published in the school newspaper arguing that the school cafeteria should change the food choices offered each day to add variety.

A letter to the editor is addressed to the editor of a newspaper or magazine. However, they are written to persuade the readers of the newspaper or magazine. They are a way for people to give their opinion to a community of people. In this case, you'll want to persuade other students, teachers, and the principal to agree with your opinion.

Notes and Ideas
Use the space below to make notes, brainstorm, or organize your ideas.

Planning Page

Use the table below to plan your writing. Then write or type your letter.

Introduction: Introduce the topic and state the main opinion.
→ Write a few sentences that tell what the topic is and state the main idea.
Supporting Ideas: Describe the reasons you will use to support the opinion.
→ Write one paragraph focused on each supporting idea.
Conclusion: Restate the main opinion and finish off the opinion piece.
→Write a paragraph that concludes your opinion piece.

Writing Prompt 78

Many people in your town ride to the local shopping mall. However, there has been an increase in the number of bikes being stolen from the mall. You believe that something needs to be done to ensure that people can safely leave their bikes at the mall. Write a letter to the editor to be published in the local newspaper arguing that the shopping mall needs more security to prevent bikes from being stolen.

You can ask yourself questions to help think of reasons to use to support your opinion. What problems does the increase in stolen bikes cause? Will it stop people going to the mall? Is it fair to people that their bikes are not being protected? Use the answers to these questions to come up with reasons that will convince people that more security is needed.

Notes and Ideas

Use the space below to make notes, brainstorm, or organize your ideas.

Planning Page

Use the table below to plan your writing. Then write or type your letter.

Introduction: Introduce the topic and state the main opinion.
→ Write a few sentences that tell what the topic is and state the main idea.
Supporting Ideas: Describe the reasons you will use to support the opinion.
→ Write one paragraph focused on each supporting idea.
Conclusion: Restate the main opinion and finish off the opinion piece.
→Write a paragraph that concludes your opinion piece.

Writing Prompt 79

You have noticed that students at your school are not attending football games as much as they used to. You believe that the football team needs students to attend to support them and cheer them on. Write a letter to the editor to be published in the school newspaper encouraging students to attend school football games.

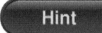

To plan your letter, start by thinking of reasons that students should attend. You could focus on how the football team needs support like the writing prompt describes. You can also think of other benefits of attending, such as describing how the games are entertaining or how it gives all students a chance to show school spirit. Brainstorm a list of reasons and then choose the most important reasons to use in your letter.

As you write the conclusion to your letter, consider including a call to action to readers. Ending with a specific action that readers should take is often a good way to finish.

Notes and Ideas

Use the space below to make notes, brainstorm, or organize your ideas.

Planning Page

Use the table below to plan your writing. Then write or type your letter.

Introduction: Introduce the topic and state the main opinion.
→ **Write a few sentences that tell what the topic is and state the main idea.**
Supporting Ideas: Describe the reasons you will use to support the opinion.
→ **Write one paragraph focused on each supporting idea.**
Conclusion: Restate the main opinion and finish off the opinion piece.
→**Write a paragraph that concludes your opinion piece.**

Writing Prompt 80

You have just read an article describing how many people waste water when it is not necessary. The article described how people water their lawns too often, choose plants that need too much water, and water their lawns during the hottest part of the day when most of the water is lost. You know that many people in your town care a lot for their lawns and gardens, and you worry that too much water is being wasted. Write a letter to the editor to be published in the local newspaper arguing that the people in your town should use water more carefully when taking care of their lawns and gardens.

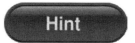

This writing prompt tells you the main ways that water is wasted when caring for lawns and gardens. You can use these ideas to give advice in your letter. However, as well as giving advice, you also need to make people care about saving water. To do this, you should show that it is important not to waste water. You can use strong language to emphasize how bad it is that water is being wasted and to show that change is needed.

Notes and Ideas

Use the space below to make notes, brainstorm, or organize your ideas.

Planning Page

Use the table below to plan your writing. Then write or type your letter.

Introduction: Introduce the topic and state the main opinion.
→ Write a few sentences that tell what the topic is and state the main idea.
Supporting Ideas: Describe the reasons you will use to support the opinion.
→ Write one paragraph focused on each supporting idea.
Conclusion: Restate the main opinion and finish off the opinion piece.
→Write a paragraph that concludes your opinion piece.

Set 17: Write a Review

Writing Prompt 81

Think of a book you have read that you liked. Write a review of the book that will persuade people to want to read it. Be sure to include details of what you liked about it.

The introduction should start with a brief summary of the book. This summary should give readers a basic idea of what type of book it is and what it is about. The introduction should end with a statement of your main idea, which is that people should read the book.

The body of the review should include details to explain why the book is worth reading. However, be sure not to retell the whole story. Instead, focus on using useful details to support your reasons for liking the book.

The conclusion should sum up your arguments and encourage people to read the book.

Notes and Ideas

Use the space below to make notes, brainstorm, or organize your ideas.

Planning Page

Use the table below to plan your writing. Then write or type your review.

Introduction: Introduce the topic and state the main opinion.
→ Write a few sentences that tell what the topic is and state the main idea.
Supporting Ideas: Describe the reasons and details you will use to support the opinion.
→ Write one paragraph focused on each supporting idea.
Conclusion: Restate the main opinion and finish off the opinion piece.
→Write a paragraph that concludes your opinion piece.

Writing Prompt 82

Think of a tourist attraction you have visited. It could be a place like the Grand Canyon, a structure or building like the Golden Gate Bridge or the Empire State Building, or a theme park like Disneyland. Write a review of the tourist attraction. Be sure to include details of what you liked or disliked about it.

A review does not have to be all positive or all negative. An honest review will often include both good and bad points. For example, a zoo might have a wide range of interesting animals and entertaining shows, but could also have long lines and poor food. You can plan your review by making a list of both good and bad points. Then choose the most important ones to focus on in your review.

Notes and Ideas

Use the space below to make notes, brainstorm, or organize your ideas.

Planning Page

Use the table below to plan your writing. Then write or type your review.

Introduction: Introduce the topic and state the main opinion.
→ Write a few sentences that tell what the topic is and state the main idea.
Supporting Ideas: Describe the reasons and details you will use to support the opinion.
→ Write one paragraph focused on each supporting idea.
Conclusion: Restate the main opinion and finish off the opinion piece.
→Write a paragraph that concludes your opinion piece.

Writing Prompt 83

Think of a meal that you recently enjoyed. It could be a meal that was cooked at home, a meal from the school cafeteria, or a meal that you ate at a restaurant or diner. Write a review of the meal. Be sure to include details of what you liked about it.

Hint

When you describe the meal, you want readers to be able to imagine what you are describing. To do this, be sure to include concrete details. These are exact and specific details. For example, don't just describe a pasta dish as delicious. This doesn't create a clear image of the meal. Instead, you might describe the generous creamy sauce that coated all the pasta. This description helps readers imagine the meal and understand what made it good.

Notes and Ideas

Use the space below to make notes, brainstorm, or organize your ideas.

Planning Page

Use the table below to plan your writing. Then write or type your review.

Introduction: Introduce the topic and state the main opinion.
→ Write a few sentences that tell what the topic is and state the main idea.
Supporting Ideas: Describe the reasons and details you will use to support the opinion.
→ Write one paragraph focused on each supporting idea.
Conclusion: Restate the main opinion and finish off the opinion piece.
→Write a paragraph that concludes your opinion piece.

Writing Prompt 84

Think of a movie you have watched that disappointed you or that you disliked. Write a review of the movie. In your review, explain what the main problems were with the movie.

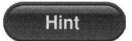

When you describe what you disliked about something, it is important to clearly state why. Be sure to think about exactly what you disliked and avoid just making vague statements. For example, you might think that the movie was boring. Do not just state that it was boring. Instead, think about exactly what made it boring. Was there not enough action? Were the characters too dull? Did it seem too long? Did nothing interesting or exciting happen? As you plan your review, focus on coming up with exact problems.

Notes and Ideas

Use the space below to make notes, brainstorm, or organize your ideas.

Planning Page

Use the table below to plan your writing. Then write or type your review.

Introduction: Introduce the topic and state the main opinion.
→ **Write a few sentences that tell what the topic is and state the main idea.**
Supporting Ideas: Describe the reasons and details you will use to support the opinion.
→ **Write one paragraph focused on each supporting idea.**
Conclusion: Restate the main opinion and finish off the opinion piece.
→**Write a paragraph that concludes your opinion piece.**

Set 18: Write a Research Piece

Writing Prompt 85

Write an article that argues that people need to drink plenty of water every day to remain healthy. Include three reasons that water is important for good health.

Use the Internet or books to look up some facts, details, or quotes that will persuade people to want to drink enough water.

The writing prompts in this section are for research pieces. This means they will be supported with facts, details, or quotes that you find. Don't worry if you don't know anything about why it is important to drink plenty of water. Unlike other types of opinion pieces, you don't need to support your main idea with personal experiences or examples you think of. Instead, you need to research to find out what other people think about the topic or what facts support the idea. You will use the information you find to support the main idea.

Notes and Ideas

Use the space below to make notes, brainstorm, or organize your ideas.

Planning Page

Use the table below to plan your writing. Then write or type your article.

Introduction: Introduce the topic and state the main opinion.
→ Write a few sentences that tell what the topic is and state the main idea.
Supporting Ideas: Describe the reasons you will use to support the opinion. Include the facts, details, or quotes you plan to use.
→ Write one paragraph focused on each supporting idea.
Conclusion: Restate the main opinion and finish off the opinion piece.
→Write a paragraph that concludes your opinion piece.

Writing Prompt 86

Many of the students at your school are starting to train for a 5-mile run to raise money for charity. Write an article that gives advice on how to train for a run without causing injury. Include details on the most common injuries and how to avoid them.

Use the Internet or books to look up some facts, details, or quotes to use in your article.

The writing prompt tells you to describe the most common injuries. To make sure your work is organized well, write about one injury in each paragraph of the body. To make the different topics clearer, you can also use subheadings to separate the information. Under each subheading, write one paragraph that describes the injury and then tells how to prevent it.

Notes and Ideas

Use the space below to make notes, brainstorm, or organize your ideas.

Planning Page

Use the table below to plan your writing. Then write or type your article.

Introduction: Introduce the topic and state the main opinion.
→ Write a few sentences that tell what the topic is and state the main idea.
Supporting Ideas: Describe the information and advice you will include. Include the facts, details, or quotes you plan to use.
→ Write one paragraph focused on each supporting idea.
Conclusion: Restate the main opinion and finish off the opinion piece.
→Write a paragraph that concludes your opinion piece.

Writing Prompt 87

Write an essay with the main idea below.

Michael Jordan was a talented basketball player who achieved a lot.

Use the Internet or books to look up some facts, details, or quotes to use in your article.

Hint

One key to doing good research is to focus on finding information that relates to your main point. You might find a lot of information about Michael Jordan. For this essay, you only need to find facts that show that he is a great basketball player. Details on where he grew up, how he started, his personal life, or even interesting facts will not support the main idea. Instead, focus on finding details about what he has achieved, records he has broken, medals or awards he has received, and what made him great.

Notes and Ideas

Use the space below to make notes, brainstorm, or organize your ideas.

Planning Page

Use the table below to plan your writing. Then write or type your essay.

Introduction: Introduce the topic and state the main opinion.
→ Write a few sentences that tell what the topic is and state the main idea.
Supporting Ideas: Describe the reasons you will use to support the opinion. Include the facts, details, or quotes you plan to use.
→ Write one paragraph focused on each supporting idea.
Conclusion: Restate the main opinion and finish off the opinion piece.
→Write a paragraph that concludes your opinion piece.

Writing Prompt 88

Write an essay with the main idea below.

> Henry Ford achieved a lot in his lifetime and is a good example of how the work of one person can have a great impact and change the world forever.

Use the Internet or books to look up some facts, details, or quotes to use in your article.

The writing prompt gives you the main argument. The main argument is not just about what Henry Ford achieved, but is also about how his work had a great impact. To support your argument, you'll need to do some research. Firstly, you can find out and write about what he achieved. Secondly, you can find out and describe why his work had a great impact and how it changed the world.

Notes and Ideas

Use the space below to make notes, brainstorm, or organize your ideas.

Planning Page

Use the table below to plan your writing. Then write or type your essay.

Introduction: Introduce the topic and state the main opinion.
→ Write a few sentences that tell what the topic is and state the main idea.
Supporting Ideas: Describe the reasons you will use to support the opinion. Include the facts, details, or quotes you plan to use.
→ Write one paragraph focused on each supporting idea.
Conclusion: Restate the main opinion and finish off the opinion piece.
→Write a paragraph that concludes your opinion piece.

Set 19: Writing to Promote

Writing Prompt 89

Imagine that a community group you are part of is holding a walkathon. The walkathon will raise money to build a new playground in a local park. The walkathon is a 5-mile walk that is designed to be fun. People are encouraged to dress up, to enter as teams, and to bring young children on the walk. Write an article for the local newspaper encouraging people to sign up for the walkathon. Be sure to give reasons that people should take part in the walkathon.

The writing prompt describes a situation you have to imagine you are in. It gives some details about the walkathon. Use these details to think of reasons that people should sign up. You can also make up any additional details about the walkathon.

Notes and Ideas
Use the space below to make notes, brainstorm, or organize your ideas.

Planning Page

Use the table below to plan your writing. Then write or type your article.

Introduction: Introduce the topic and state your main purpose.
→ **Write a few sentences that tell what the topic is and state what you want readers to do.**
Supporting Ideas: Describe the reasons you will use to persuade readers.
→ **Write one paragraph focused on each reason.**
Conclusion: Restate the main purpose and finish off the opinion piece.
→**Write a paragraph that concludes your opinion piece.**

Writing Prompt 90

You are part of the school's track and field team. Team members compete in events including running, hurdles, long jump, high jump, shot put, and javelin. The team needs more members to take part in these events. Write a letter for the school newspaper encouraging people to join the track and field team. Be sure to include reasons that students should join the team.

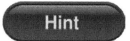

Your letter should give reasons that people should join the team. As you think of reasons that students should join, think about what track and field might be like and what students might gain from it. For example, do you think it would be fun? Could it be challenging? Could students discover a new talent? Could students have the chance to win competitions? You can decide what you think the main benefits of joining would be. Just be sure to clearly describe these benefits in a way that will make students want to join the track and field team.

Notes and Ideas
Use the space below to make notes, brainstorm, or organize your ideas.

Planning Page

Use the table below to plan your writing. Then write or type your letter.

Introduction: Introduce the topic and state your main purpose.
→ **Write a few sentences that tell what the topic is and state what you want readers to do.**
Supporting Ideas: Describe the reasons you will use to persuade readers.
→ Write one paragraph focused on each reason.
Conclusion: Restate the main purpose and finish off the opinion piece.
→Write a paragraph that concludes your opinion piece.

Writing Prompt 91

You are part of a group of students helping to organize the school talent show. The talent show wants students with a wide range of talents such as singing, dancing, acting, doing magic, or performing comedy. You are worried that not enough students want to try out for the talent show. Write an article for the school newspaper encouraging students to try out. Include three reasons that students should try out.

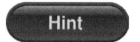

A call to action is a statement that encourages readers to take some action right away. In opinion pieces trying to persuade readers to do something, it is a good idea to include calls to action in the conclusion. A great call to action will tell readers exactly what to do and have a positive tone that makes readers want to take action.

Notes and Ideas

Use the space below to make notes, brainstorm, or organize your ideas.

Planning Page

Use the table below to plan your writing. Then write or type your article.

Introduction: Introduce the topic and state your main purpose.   → **Write a few sentences that tell what the topic is and state what you want readers to do.**
Supporting Ideas: Describe the reasons you will use to persuade readers.   → **Write one paragraph focused on each reason.**
Conclusion: Restate the main purpose and finish off the opinion piece.   →**Write a paragraph that concludes your opinion piece.**

Writing Prompt 92

Imagine that a local animal shelter has many cats and dogs that need to be adopted. You want to encourage people to consider adopting a dog or cat. Create a flyer to hand out to students that encourages people to consider adopting a pet from the shelter.

A flyer does not have to have as much writing as a letter or article, but it should still have a main idea, supporting ideas, and a conclusion. The main idea will be what you want people who read the flyer to do. In this case, the main idea is that people should consider adopting a cat or dog from the shelter. The supporting ideas will be the reasons that people should. The conclusion could be a summary of your main points or a call to action.

Notes and Ideas

Use the space below to make notes, brainstorm, or organize your ideas.

Planning Page

Use the table below to plan your writing. Then write or type your flyer.

Introduction: Introduce the topic and state your main purpose.
→ Write a few sentences that tell what the topic is and state what you want readers to do.
Supporting Ideas: Describe the reasons you will use to persuade readers.
→ Write one paragraph focused on each reason.
Conclusion: Restate the main purpose and finish off the opinion piece.
→Write a paragraph that concludes your opinion piece.

Set 20: Write a Response to Literature

Writing Prompt 93

Read the passage below. Then answer the questions about the passage.

A Man's Best Friend
by Damon Navarro

My dog is always smiling,
Come rain, hail, or shine.
His tail is always wagging,
Whether night or morning time.

He wakes me in the morning,
With the brush of his wet nose,
And lies beneath the covers,
Curled up tight beside my toes.

We go on winding morning walks,
Across the sunlit grounds,
He sniffs the scent of every plant,
And takes in every sound.

He enjoys everything around him,
With an endless sense of wonder,
And is not scared of anything,
Not rain, not noise, not thunder.

Whether running through the fields,
Or playing with his toys,
He is a ray of constant sunshine,
And an endless source of joy.

1   The author describes what his dog is like. Do you think most dogs are similar to the dog described? Explain your answer.

_____

_____

_____

_____

_____

_____

2   What do you think is the main reason the author finds his dog "an endless source of joy"? Use details from the passage to support your answer.

_____

_____

_____

_____

_____

_____

3 Many people like having a pet dog because it is enjoyable to spend time with the dog. Write an article for the school newspaper arguing that dogs are enjoyable pets to own. Use details from the passage and your own ideas to support your answer.

Use the table below to plan your work. Then write an article of 1 to 2 pages.

Introduction: Introduce the topic and state the main opinion.
→ Write a few sentences that tell what the topic is and state the main idea.
Supporting Ideas: Describe the reasons and details you will use to support the opinion.
→ Write one paragraph focused on each supporting idea.
Conclusion: Restate the main opinion and finish off the opinion piece.
→Write a paragraph that concludes your opinion piece.

Writing Prompt 94

Read the passage below. Then answer the questions about the passage.

Bruce and the Spider

There was once a king of Scotland whose name was Robert Bruce. He had need to be both brave and wise, for the times in which he lived were tough. The King of England was at war with him, and had led a great army into Scotland to drive him out of the land.

Battle after battle had been fought. Bruce led his brave little army against his foes six times, and six times his men had been beaten and driven into flight. At last his army was scattered, and he was forced to hide himself in the woods and in lonely places among the mountains.

One rainy day, Bruce lay on the ground under a shed, listening to the patter of the drops on the roof above him. He was tired and sick at heart, and ready to give up all hope. It seemed to him that there was no use for him to try to do anything more.

As he lay thinking, he saw a spider over his head, making ready to weave her web. He watched her as she toiled slowly and with great care. Six times she tried to throw her frail thread from one beam to another, and six times it fell short.

"Poor thing!" said Bruce. "You, too, know what it is to fail."

But the spider did not lose hope with the sixth failure. With still more care, she made ready to try for the seventh time. Bruce almost forgot his own troubles as he watched her swing herself out upon the slender line. Would she fail again? No! The thread was carried safely to the beam, and fastened there.

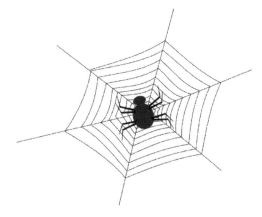

"I, too, will try a seventh time!" cried Bruce.

He arose and called his men together. He told them of his plans, and sent them out with messages of cheer to his disheartened people. Soon there was an army of brave men around him. Another battle was fought, and the King of England was glad to go back into his own country.

I have heard it said, that, after that day, no one by the name of Bruce would ever hurt a spider. The lesson which the little creature had taught the king was never forgotten.

1 In the third paragraph, the author describes how Bruce was "ready to give up all hope." Is it understandable that Bruce felt this way? Use details from the passage to support your answer.

_____

_____

_____

_____

_____

_____

2 Think about how the men Bruce was in charge of would have felt. Is it fair for a king to give up? Explain your answer.

_____

_____

_____

_____

_____

_____

3 The passage has a lesson about not giving up even when you feel like you have lost hope. Is the lesson important mainly for leaders like the King of Scotland or is it just as important for all people? Use details from the passage and your own ideas and experiences to support your answer.

Use the table below to plan your work. Then write an essay of 1 to 2 pages.

Introduction: Introduce the topic and state the main opinion.   → Write a few sentences that tell what the topic is and state the main idea.
Supporting Ideas: Describe the reasons and details you will use to support the opinion.   → Write one paragraph focused on each supporting idea.
Conclusion: Restate the main opinion and finish off the opinion piece.   →Write a paragraph that concludes your opinion piece.

Writing Prompt 95

Read the passage below. Then answer the questions about the passage.

Taking the Lead

Thomas was a very competitive person. He always did his utmost to win every game, race, or challenge. His favorite sport was athletics. Ever since he had been a child, he had enjoyed sprinting. He had won a number of events at the last regional sports day. Thomas represented his school regularly. He also trained very hard for each and every event. He took his preparation very seriously. He dreamed that one day he would be a professional athlete competing in the Olympic Games.

His attitude, however, didn't win him many friends. He sometimes insulted fellow competitors by laughing when they lost. On the rare occasions Thomas lost, he did not shake his rival's hand or congratulate anyone who had finished ahead of him. Both his parents and his teachers told him that part of winning was learning how to also lose with grace. Despite this, he chose to ignore their advice and continue along the same paths as before. Many of Thomas' peers disliked his behavior. They wished he would be more thoughtful towards his fellow competitors.

One day, Thomas was in a race against a rival school. They were competing for the top regional trophy. In the first event, Thomas had won but suffered a small strain to his right knee. His coach and the team doctor examined the injury and suggested that he sit out of the final race. Thomas refused to listen to their suggestions.

"You should sit this out," explained his doctor carefully. "If you race, you may not only lose but you could make the injury worse."

Thomas shook his head.

"I am fine. If I don't race our school has *no* chance of winning."

Thomas' teammates were insulted by his statement. However, Thomas was allowed to compete. When the race started, Thomas decided to set off at a very quick pace. This was unusual as he liked to pace himself and finish strong at the close of the race. His injury inspired him to start quickly and get a solid lead. After the first lap, he was far in front of everyone else. His lead actually increased over the next lap, too. Then it happened. He felt a sharp and sudden pain in his knee before he felt himself starting to fall. He tried to regain his balance but his injured knee couldn't hold him any longer.

Thomas came last in the race and had to be carried off the track. He was very quiet as he lay still in the changing rooms.

"You've strained your knee quite badly," said the doctor. "You will need to rest it for a few weeks."

Thomas looked at his teammates looking on.

"I am sorry," he said to his teammates as they gathered around him. "I let you all down."

He expected his teammates to be mad at him, but they only seemed concerned about his health. Thomas imagined what he might have done if someone else in the team had tried to run with an injury. He imagined that he would be furious. He suddenly realized how selfish he had been. From that day forward, Thomas vowed to be a better sportsman and use his competitive nature to benefit his team.

1 In the first paragraph, the author describes how impressive Thomas is. What impresses you most about Thomas? Explain your answer.

2 Think about how Thomas's teammates reacted in the last paragraph. Were you surprised by how they reacted? Explain why or why not.

3 Write an article for the school newspaper with the main idea below.

While winning is the goal in sports, it is also important to think of other people.

Use details from the passage and your own ideas to support your answer.

Use the table below to plan your work. Then write an article of 1 to 2 pages.

Introduction: Introduce the topic and state the main opinion.
→ **Write a few sentences that tell what the topic is and state the main idea.**
Supporting Ideas: Describe the reasons and details you will use to support the opinion.
→ **Write one paragraph focused on each supporting idea.**
Conclusion: Restate the main opinion and finish off the opinion piece.
→**Write a paragraph that concludes your opinion piece.**

Writing Prompt 96

Read the passage below. Then answer the questions about the passage.

Saving the Birds

One day in spring four men were riding on horseback along a country road. These men were lawyers, and they were going to the next town to attend court.

There had been rain, and the ground was very soft. Water was dripping from the trees, and the grass was wet.

The four lawyers rode along, one behind another; for the pathway was narrow, and the mud on each side of it was deep. They rode slowly, and talked and laughed and were very jolly.

As they were passing through a grove of small trees, they heard a great fluttering over their heads and a feeble chirping in the grass by the roadside.

"What is the matter here?" asked the first lawyer, whose name was Speed.

"Oh, it's only some old robins!" said the second lawyer, whose name was Hardin. "The storm has blown two of the little ones out of the nest. They are too young to fly, and the mother bird is making a great fuss about it."

"What a pity! They'll die down there in the grass," said the third lawyer.

"Oh, well! They're nothing but birds," said Hardin. "Why should we bother?"

"Yes, why should we?" said Speed.

The three men, as they passed, looked down and saw the little birds fluttering in the cold, wet grass. They saw the mother robin flying about, and crying to her mate.

Then they rode on, talking and laughing as before.

But the fourth lawyer, whose name was Abraham Lincoln, stopped. He got down from his horse and very gently took the little ones up in his big warm hands. They did not seem frightened, but chirped softly, as if they knew they were safe.

"Never mind, my little fellows," said Lincoln. "I will put you in your own cozy little bed."

Then he looked up to find the nest from which they had fallen. It was much higher than he could reach. But Lincoln could climb. He had climbed many a tree when he was a boy. He put the birds softly, one by one, into their warm little home. All cuddled down together and were very happy.

Soon the three lawyers who had ridden ahead stopped at a spring to give their horses water.

In a few minutes Lincoln joined them. His shoes were covered with mud and he had torn his coat on the thorny tree.

"Hello, Abraham!" said Hardin. "Where have you been?"

"I stopped a minute to give those birds to their mother," he answered.

"Well, we always thought you were a hero," said Speed. "Now we know it."

Then all three of them laughed heartily. They thought it so foolish that a strong man should take so much trouble just for some worthless young birds.

"Gentlemen," said Lincoln, "I could not have slept tonight, if I had left those helpless little robins to perish in the wet grass."

Abraham Lincoln afterwards became very famous as a lawyer, statesman, and as President of the United States.

1   Hardin can be described as mean. Give two details from the passage that support the idea that he is mean.

    1. _____

    _____

    _____

    2. _____

    _____

    _____

2   How do you think Lincoln would have felt after helping the birds? Use details from the passage to support your answer.

    _____

    _____

    _____

    _____

    _____

    _____

3 Hardin and Speed did not think it was worth saving the birds, but Lincoln did. Do you think saving the birds was worth the trouble? Write an essay giving your opinion. Use details from the passage to support your answer.

Use the table below to plan your work. Then write an essay of 1 to 2 pages.

Introduction: Introduce the topic and state the main opinion.
→ **Write a few sentences that tell what the topic is and state the main idea.**
Supporting Ideas: Describe the reasons and details you will use to support the opinion.
→ **Write one paragraph focused on each supporting idea.**
Conclusion: Restate the main opinion and finish off the opinion piece.
→**Write a paragraph that concludes your opinion piece.**

Set 21: Write a Response to Informational Texts

Writing Prompt 97

Read the passage below. Then answer the questions about the passage.

The Loch Ness Monster

The Loch Ness Monster is a creature that is reported to live in Loch Ness, a lake in the Scottish Highlands. The picture on the right is a model showing what it is thought to look like. However, it has never actually been proven to exist.

There have been several thousands of reported sightings since 1930. However, any examples of photographs or videos that have been offered have not been accepted by experts. Modern scientists believe the Loch Ness Monster to be a myth. They claim that any sightings are either hoaxes or the results of wishful thinking. Another school of thought suggests that the Loch Ness Monster does exist and is in fact a survivor of the dinosaur age.

This theory also applies to similar creatures that have been sighted in other Scottish lakes. It suggests that the Loch Ness Monster is part of the long-surviving plesiosaurs family. These were meat-eating breeds of reptile that first emerged millions of years ago. Their physical appearance fits the typical description of the Loch Ness Monster and also many of the images captured by camera. Despite this, scientists claim that the plesiosaurs family became extinct thousands of years ago. Many consider the Loch Ness Monster to be just a legend or a tall tale.

Believers considered that a breakthrough had been made in 2007. At this time, a man named Gordon Holmes captured a detailed video of what he described to be the Loch Ness Monster. He claimed to have filmed a 14-meter long creature moving quickly beneath the surface of the water.

Holmes submitted the tape to a marine biologist. After an initial review, it was described as the best footage that had been recorded since the turn of the century. Many considered that it may offer final proof that the Loch Ness Monster exists.

However, a closer look at the tape raised some serious concerns. It was thought that the creature captured on film was likely to be a sea otter or water bird. Gordon Holmes himself then became the subject of discussion. Many believed that he had faked the footage. He was known to have a long history of sighting mythical creatures and fairies. This mistrust of the evidence suggests that even modern technology will be unable to confirm whether the Loch Ness Monster is a real creature.

Various expeditions have been led to search for the monster since 1962. The most recent of these was carried out by the BBC in 2003. In this study, 600 separate solar beams and satellites were used to track any motion in the water. Despite the advanced technology, no large or unusual animal was detected throughout the search. It is believed that the failure of this expedition is the final proof that the Loch Ness Monster is only a myth.

© Sam Fentress, Wikimedia Commons

1 Imagine it is discovered that the Loch Ness Monster is real. Do you think this would be an exciting find? Explain your answer.

_____

_____

_____

_____

_____

_____

2 Was it fair to Gordon that people did not believe his video footage of the Loch Ness Monster was real? Use details from the passage to support your answer.

_____

_____

_____

_____

_____

_____

3 The Loch Ness Monster has interested people for decades. Other mysterious creatures like the Yeti also fascinate people. Why do you think people are so interested in unknown creatures? Write an essay giving your opinion. Use details from the passage and your own ideas in your answer.

Use the table below to plan your work. Then write an essay of 1 to 2 pages.

Introduction: Introduce the topic and state the main opinion.
→ Write a few sentences that tell what the topic is and state the main idea.
Supporting Ideas: Describe the reasons and details you will use to support the opinion.
→ Write one paragraph focused on each supporting idea.
Conclusion: Restate the main opinion and finish off the opinion piece.
→Write a paragraph that concludes your opinion piece.

Writing Prompt 98

Read the passage below. Then answer the questions about the passage.

Start a Lemonade Stand

Do you want an easy way to make some extra money on the weekend? Make a nice big batch of lemonade and start a lemonade stand in your front yard. Here are some tips for setting up a good lemonade stand.

Location, Location, Location

Make sure you have a good spot. You're usually not allowed to set up stands in public places like parks, so you'll need to do it in your yard. But it's best if you live in a spot where plenty of people will walk past. If your home is not right, consider asking a friend who lives in a better spot to help you. Then you can set up the stand at your friend's house.

Get Noticed

Get your stand noticed. You want your stand to be easy to spot. Take the time to paint a colorful banner or to put up signs. You can also add things like streamers and balloons. You could also put signs up at the end of your street. Then people will know that fresh lemonade is just around the corner.

Price it Right

Choose the right price. You need to make sure you aren't charging too much for your lemonade. It's also easiest if you don't need to worry about giving change. Set your price to $1, $2, or $3. You should also be willing to do deals. If someone wants to buy more than one, offer them a special deal.

Looks are Important

You want people to want to drink your lemonade, so make sure you present it nicely. You can add a few lemon wedges to the container to make it look nice and fresh. You can also place lemons around your stand as decorations. You should also cover the table you are using with a nice tablecloth. The nicer your stand looks, the more people will want to buy your product.

Offer More than Lemonade

Add other products. Do you have a friend who makes delicious cupcakes or amazing banana bread? Invite them to join in. You can sell treats to go with your fresh lemonade and make even more money.

1 The author states that a lemonade stand is "an easy way to make some extra money on the weekend." Do you agree with this statement? Use details from the passage to support your answer.

_____

_____

_____

_____

_____

_____

2 In the section "Looks are Important," the author describes how to make the lemonade and the lemonade stand look good. Do you think this would make people more likely to buy lemonade? Explain why or why not.

_____

_____

_____

_____

_____

_____

3 The author gives a lot of advice about how to start a lemonade stand. Which three pieces of advice do you think are most important? Write an essay explaining why that advice is important. Use details from the passage to support your answer.

Use the table below to plan your work. Then write an essay of 1 to 2 pages.

Introduction: Introduce the topic and state the main opinion.
→ **Write a few sentences that tell what the topic is and state the main idea.**
Supporting Ideas: Describe the reasons and details you will use to support the opinion.
→ **Write one paragraph focused on each supporting idea.**
Conclusion: Restate the main opinion and finish off the opinion piece.
→**Write a paragraph that concludes your opinion piece.**

Writing Prompt 99

Read the passage below. Then answer the questions about the passage.

Be Prepared

The Scouts is a worldwide youth movement aimed at supporting the physical and mental development of young males. The Scouts was started in 1907 by Robert Baden-Powell, who was a Lieutenant General in the British Army.

During the 1900s, the movement grew to include three different age groups of boys. The Cub Scouts is for boys aged from 7 to 11. The Scouts is for boys aged 11 to 18. The Rover Scouts is for boys aged over 18. In 1910, a similar organization was created for girls. It is known as the Girl Guides. The motto of the Scouts is "Be Prepared." The aim of the Scouts is not just to promote fitness, but to build character. By taking part in a range of activities, members learn important personal skills.

One of the key features of the Scouts is that members earn merit badges as they develop new skills. Once each badge is earned, the patch for the badge can be added to the uniform.

Bird Study, Fire Safety, Plant Science, Rowing, First Aid, Cooking, Camping, and Public Speaking are some of the badges that can be earned.

In 1911, an official handbook for the Boy Scouts of America was published. This introduction to the book encourages readers to join the scouts.

> "Scout" used to mean the one on watch for the rest. We have widened the word a little. We have made it fit the town as well as the wilderness and suited it to peace time instead of war. We have made the scout an expert in Life-craft as well as Wood-craft, for he is trained in the things of the heart as well as head and hand. Scouting we have made to cover riding, swimming, tramping, trailing, photography, first aid, camping, handicraft, loyalty, obedience, courtesy, thrift, courage, and kindness.
>
> Do these things appeal to you? Do you love the woods? Do you wish to learn the trees as the forester knows them? And the stars not as an astronomer, but as a traveler?
>
> Do you wish to have all-round, well-developed muscles, not those of a great athlete, but those of a sound body that will not fail you? Would you like to be an expert camper who can always make himself comfortable out of doors, and a swimmer that fears no waters? Do you desire the knowledge to help the wounded quickly, and to make yourself cool and self-reliant in an emergency?
>
> Do you believe in loyalty, courage, and kindness? Would you like to form habits that will surely make your success in life?
>
> Then, whether you be farm boy or shoe clerk, newsboy or millionaire's son, your place is in our ranks, for these are the thoughts in scouting. It will help you to do better work with your pigs, your shoes, your papers, or your dollars. It will give you new pleasures in life. It will teach you so much of the outdoor world that you wish to know.

Even though this introduction was written over one hundred years ago, it still describes what the Scouts are about today. It is about learning a wide range of skills that will prepare you for all kinds of situations. You will learn new things, experience new things, and have the kinds of abilities that will serve you well throughout your life.

1   The passage describes how people earn merit badges. Do you think earning badges would motivate people to learn new skills? Explain your answer.

   _____

   _____

   _____

   _____

   _____

   _____

2   Would the introduction from 1911 convince you to join the Scouts? Explain why or why not.

   _____

   _____

   _____

   _____

   _____

   _____

3 How would being a member of the Scouts help prepare you for life? Write an article for the school newspaper arguing that being in the Scouts develops important life skills. Include three examples of life skills that would be learned. Use details from the passage to support your answer.

Use the table below to plan your work. Then write an article of 1 to 2 pages.

Introduction: Introduce the topic and state the main opinion.
→ Write a few sentences that tell what the topic is and state the main idea.
Supporting Ideas: Describe the examples and details you will use to support the opinion.
→ Write one paragraph focused on each supporting idea.
Conclusion: Restate the main opinion and finish off the opinion piece.
→Write a paragraph that concludes your opinion piece.

Writing Prompt 100

Read the passage below. Then answer the questions about the passage.

The Discovery of Gold in California

In 1847, California had a population of less than 10,000 people. Then a remarkable event occurred. Captain Sutter had settled on the Sacramento River and built a sawmill. In January, 1848, one of Sutter's laborers, by the name of Marshall, while digging a ditch for the mill, found shiny pieces of yellow metal which they suspected might be gold.

"I wonder what that yellow stuff is," said he. "I wonder if it is gold."

"I reckon it is brass," said one of his helpers.

"Let me try vinegar on it," said Marshall. It was tried and the vinegar did not affect the "yellow stuff."

The men threw down their tools and went to work searching for gold. Mr. Sutter laughed at the idea. But gold indeed it was, and there was plenty of it!

The news spread. Soon everybody knew that pure gold was found and in wonderful quantities. What a rush there was to the "diggings"! How all sorts of people from all over the western coast crowded in! Doctors left their sick, ministers their pulpits, traders their shops, mechanics their tools, and farmers their fields, all half frantic with the desire to dig their fortunes out of the golden sands of California.

When the news of the discovery of gold reached the East, many people seemed to catch the contagion. Multitudes started at once for California. Thousands came by long wagon trains over the dreary plains. Vast numbers came from foreign countries. Even the crews and often the officers abandoned the ships that brought crowds to the Pacific coast and started for the gold "diggings."

The rush to the gold fields began in 1848, but became enormous in 1849. Those who went that year are since called "Forty-niners." There were over eighty thousand of them! The crowds that thronged the gold regions dug up the country for miles around Sutter's mill. They tore up his beautiful valley and ruined his farm. But they soon learned that gold was also to be found in larger quantities along the streams, among the mountains, and in valleys.

Month by month new-comers swarmed in, and the excitement grew more intense. Some found prizes, nuggets of solid gold as large as an acorn or a walnut, and at times masses two or three pounds in weight. However much gold a man found, he was wildly eager to get more.

A great deal of suffering ensued from the scarcity of food and the enormous prices of everything. Potatoes sold for a dollar apiece, eggs at the same price, wood at fifty dollars a cord, and flour at a hundred dollars a barrel. Large butcher knives were found very useful for digging, and brought thirty dollars each. A dose of the cheapest medicine cost five dollars, and a physician's visit a hundred dollars. Unskilled laborers were paid twenty-five dollars a day.

Money was not used at the mines, but in its place the ore itself, or "dust," at about sixteen dollars an ounce. Miners carried small scales, weighed their gold dust, and paid their bills with it.

At the rough log tavern: "What do you charge for dinner here?" "Half an ounce."

At the wayside store: "What's the price of these boots?" "Three ounces."

In seven years' time, from 1849 to 1856, the gold found in California was worth nearly five hundred million dollars!

California is still rich in its gold, but it is still richer in its wonderful climate and its marvelous scenery; in the wealth of its grain fields; its sheep and cattle; its orange groves and its vineyards. These make California the real land of gold, and ensure the prosperity and happiness of its people.

1   The author describes how people gave up their jobs to travel to the gold fields. Do you think this was wise? Explain why or why not.

_____

_____

_____

_____

_____

_____

2   Do you think digging for gold in California would have been mostly exciting or mostly frustrating? Use details from the passage to explain your answer.

_____

_____

_____

_____

_____

_____

3 Write an essay that supports the statement below.

>The discovery of gold in California was not all positive. Instead, it caused many problems.

In your essay, describe three problems that occurred. Use details from the passage to support your answer.

Use the table below to plan your work. Then write an essay of 1 to 2 pages.

Introduction: Introduce the topic and state the main opinion.
→ **Write a few sentences that tell what the topic is and state the main idea.**
Supporting Ideas: Describe the reasons and details you will use to support the opinion.
→ **Write one paragraph focused on each supporting idea.**
Conclusion: Restate the main opinion and finish off the opinion piece.
→**Write a paragraph that concludes your opinion piece.**

WRITING REVIEW AND SCORING GUIDE
For Parents, Teachers, and Tutors

Each set of writing prompts is designed to help students focus on one aspect of persuasive writing or one type of opinion piece. The scoring guides below list key factors that should be considered when reviewing writing tasks in each set.

After students have completed each writing task, review their work based on the factors listed. Identify strengths, weaknesses, and changes that can be made to improve their work. Give students guidance on what to focus on in the next writing task to improve their score.

Developing Writing Skills

Warm-Up Exercise: Best and Worst Qualities

The student should complete each statement by naming a best or worst quality. The student should provide one or more reasons that support the statement. Any answer can be accepted as long as it states an opinion and includes valid reasons.

Set 1: Stating an Opinion

The student should complete the table by stating the opinion and briefly describing the supporting ideas. The information in the table should be used to write a short opinion piece.

Review the student's opinion piece based on the key factors listed below.
- Does it start by clearly stating the main idea?
- Does it include reasonable supporting ideas?
- Are the supporting ideas clearly related to the main idea?
- Is the opinion piece based on the plan from the table?

Warm-Up Exercise: Using Sequence Words

The student should write a paragraph telling someone he or she enjoys spending time with and something he or she enjoys doing. Each paragraph should include a statement of the main idea. Each paragraph should include three reasons to explain why. The reasons should be introduced using the words and phrases in the order below.
1. For one thing, / As well as that, / Finally,
2. To begin with, / Additionally, / Lastly

Set 2: Organizing Your Ideas

Review the student's opinion piece based on the key factors listed below.
- Does the first paragraph introduce the topic and state the main idea?
- Is the main idea clearly stated?
- Does it include one paragraph for each of the three supporting ideas?
- Is each paragraph focused on the supporting idea?
- Does it include a conclusion that restates the main idea?

Warm-Up Exercise: Pros and Cons

The student should complete each table with pros and cons for the topic given. Any reasonable answers can be accepted.

Set 3: Listing and Choosing Supporting Ideas

The student should list supporting ideas for each opinion. The student should select one of the supporting ideas and write a paragraph that supports the opinion based on that idea. The paragraph should be clearly focused on the supporting idea selected.

Warm-Up Exercise: Stating Main Ideas

The student should complete each sentence with an opinion on the selected topic. Any reasonable answers can be accepted.

Set 4: Introducing the Topic

Review the student's opinion piece based on the key factors listed below.
- Does the first paragraph introduce the topic well?
- Is the topic of the opinion piece clear?
- Will the description of the topic help readers understand the issue?
- Is any necessary background information included?
- Is the main idea clearly stated at the end of the introduction?
- Does the body include reasonable supporting ideas?
- Is each paragraph of the body focused on one supporting idea?
- Does it include a conclusion that restates the main idea?

Warm-Up Exercise: Choosing a Title

The student should provide three alternative titles for each simple title given. Each title should relate to the same main idea, but should also catch the reader's attention in some way. Possible techniques used could include asking questions, making a demand, writing an interesting or catchy statement, using rhyme or onomatopoeia, using humor, or using strong language.

Set 5: Starting Strong

The student should complete the activity listed to help plan the introduction. The student should then write an introduction using the technique described.

Review the student's introduction based on the key factors listed below.
- Does the introduction use the technique described?
- Is the introduction effective?
- Does the introduction get the reader's attention?
- Is the topic of the opinion piece clear?
- Is the main idea clearly stated?

Warm-Up Exercise: Using Concrete Details

The student should list three concrete details for each vague detail given. Each concrete detail should relate to the vague detail given. Concrete details may give specific information, describe something that is relevant, create a clear image, or use sensory details.

Set 6: Using Details to Support an Opinion

Review the student's opinion piece based on the key factors listed below.
- Does the first paragraph introduce the topic and state the main idea?
- Is the main idea clearly stated?
- Does the body include one paragraph for each reason or supporting idea?
- Is each paragraph focused on the reason or supporting idea?
- Does each paragraph include relevant details?
- Do the details included make the meaning clearer?
- Does it include a conclusion that restates the main idea?

Warm-Up Exercise: Choosing a Topic

The student should list three or four topics based on the general idea given. Each topic should relate the general idea to a specific situation, issue, or subject. Any reasonable answers can be accepted.

Set 7: Using Examples to Support an Opinion

Review the student's opinion piece based on the key factors listed below.
- Does the first paragraph introduce the topic and state the main idea?
- Is the main idea clearly stated?
- Does the body include three examples as supporting ideas?
- Is each paragraph focused on one example?
- Are the examples relevant?
- Do the examples support the main idea well?
- Are the examples clearly described?
- Does it include a conclusion that restates the main idea?

Warm-Up Exercise: Personal Experiences and Meaning

The student should complete each chart by describing a personal experience that relates to the main idea given. The experiences described should help show that the main idea is true.

Set 8: Using Personal Experience to Support an Opinion

Writing Prompt 41
The student should describe a personal experience that relates to the opinion given. The experience described should clearly support the opinion.

Writing Prompts 42, 43, and 44
The student should list three situations that relate to the opinion given. Each situation should clearly support the opinion. The student should select one situation, describe it, and give a reasonable explanation of how it supports the opinion.

Writing Prompt 45
Review the student's opinion piece based on the key factors listed below.
- Does the first paragraph introduce the topic and state the main idea?
- Is the main idea clearly stated?
- Is the main idea supported by a personal experience?
- Is the personal experience clearly described?
- Does the personal experience effectively support the main idea?
- Does it include a conclusion that restates the main idea?

Warm-Up Exercise: Using Linking Words and Phrases

The student should complete each sentence in a way that makes sense. Any reasonable answer can be accepted. Sample answers are given below.

1   Most jobs require good computer skills, <u>so</u> everyone should take a computer course.

2   There are only 40 bike racks, but over one hundred students ride to school. <u>Therefore</u>, the school needs to add a lot more bike racks.

3   The basketball team train the hardest and have the best coach. <u>Consequently</u>, they are leading the competition this year.

4   <u>As a result</u> of the high cost of going to the camp, many students are looking for other camps they can attend.

5   There is more graffiti appearing at the school. <u>In order to</u> stop this, more lighting is going to be added.

6   Not all dogs that appear friendly really are. <u>For this reason</u>, it is important not to try to pat a dog without asking the owner first.

Set 9: Using Facts to Support an Opinion

The student should list three facts that support each main idea given. The facts listed should be accurate and relevant. The student should then use the three facts to write a complete paragraph. The paragraph should state the main idea and use the facts to support the main idea effectively.

Warm-Up Exercise: Introducing the Conclusion

The student should reword each statement. Each answer should keep about the same meaning and should be suitable for use in a conclusion. Any reasonable answer can be accepted. Sample answers are given below.

1. As you can see, change is not something that needs to be feared.
2. Becoming angry only makes things worse, so it is important to remain calm.
3. It must now be clear that water is precious and must not be wasted.
4. Winter storms are sure to occur, so it is important to be prepared for them.
5. Overall, movies today do not have the same humor that they used to.
6. Exercise should be enjoyed and should never feel like a bother.

Set 10: Writing the Conclusion

The student should write a one-paragraph conclusion based on the main idea and supporting ideas given.

Review the student's conclusion based on the key factors listed below.
- Does it state the main idea clearly?
- Is the main idea effectively reworded?
- Are the supporting ideas summarized and restated?
- Does it finish in an effective way?

Warm-Up Exercise: Using Strong Language

Students should replace the underlined words in each sentence with a stronger word or phrase. The word or phrase should not change the meaning of the sentence, but should make the meaning clearer or have a greater impact. Any reasonable answer can be accepted. Sample answers are given below.

1. exhausted
2. am certain that / tastier
3. unacceptable
4. greatly overpriced
5. urge / seriously consider

Set 11: Using Calls to Action

Writing Prompt 56

The student should write an effective ending to the paragraph that includes a call to action.

Writing Prompts 57 to 60

The student should make notes to help plan the conclusion. The student should then complete the conclusion with a call to action.

Review the student's conclusion based on the key factors listed below.
- Does the conclusion use a call to action?
- Does the call to action address the reader and ask for a suitable action to be taken?
- Does the call to action include a reason to take action or describe a result of taking action?
- Is the call to action effective and convincing?

Applying Writing Skills

Sets 12 to 19

Use the Opinion Piece Scoring Rubric at the end of the book to score each opinion piece out of 20.

Sets 20 to 21

Use the Short Answer Scoring Rubric at the end of the book to score the first two questions out of 10.

Use the Opinion Piece Scoring Rubric at the end of the book to score the third question out of 20.

SHORT ANSWER SCORING RUBRIC

This writing rubric describes the features that are expected in student writing. Give students a score out of 2 for each aspect listed below. Then combine the scores to give a total score out of 10. Students can also be given feedback and guidance based on the criteria below.

	Score	Notes
Reading Comprehension To receive a full score, the response will: • show comprehension of the text • address the question effectively		
Purpose, Focus, and Organization To receive a full score, the response will: • maintain a clear focus • be organized effectively		
Evidence and Elaboration To receive a full score, the response will: • use clear reasoning • include reasonable explanations • use suitable supporting details from the text, when required		
Written Expression To receive a full score, the response will: • be clear and easy to understand • have good transitions between ideas • use language to communicate ideas clearly		
Writing Conventions To receive a full score, the response will: • have few or no spelling errors • have few or no grammar errors • have few or no capitalization errors • have few or no punctuation errors		
Total Score		

OPINION PIECE SCORING RUBRIC

This writing rubric describes the features that are expected in student writing. Give students a score out of 5 for each aspect listed below. Then combine the scores to give a total score out of 20. Students can also be given feedback and guidance based on the criteria below.

	Score	Notes
Purpose, Focus, and Organization To receive a full score, the response will: • have an opening that introduces the topic and clearly states an opinion • maintain a clear focus throughout the piece • contain little or no irrelevant information • have an effective structure that includes an introduction, body, and conclusion • have a well-organized body with related information grouped together • provide a concluding statement or section		
Evidence and Elaboration To receive a full score, the response will: • provide reasons to support the opinion • include clearly stated supporting ideas • effectively use facts, details, or examples to support ideas • use relevant text-based evidence when appropriate		
Written Expression To receive a full score, the response will: • be clear and easy to understand • have good transitions between ideas • use language to communicate ideas clearly • use writing techniques effectively • have varied sentence structures		
Writing Conventions To receive a full score, the response will: • have few or no spelling errors • have few or no grammar errors • have few or no capitalization errors • have few or no punctuation errors		
Total Score		

Get to Know Our Product Range

Mathematics

Practice Test Books
Practice sets and practice tests will prepare students for the state tests.

Quiz Books
Focused individual quizzes cover every math skill one by one.

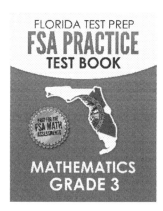 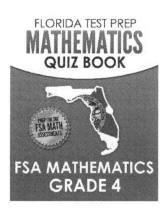 

Reading

Practice Test Books
Practice sets and practice tests will prepare students for the state tests.

Reading Skills Workbooks
Short passages and question sets will develop and improve reading comprehension skills and are perfect for ongoing test prep.

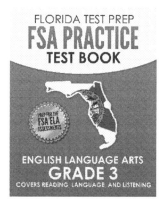 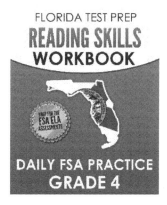 

Writing

Writing Skills Workbooks
Students write narratives, essays, and opinion pieces, and write in response to passages.

Persuasive and Narrative Writing Workbooks
Guided workbooks teach all the skills required to write effective narratives and opinion pieces.

Language

Language Quiz Books
Focused quizzes cover spelling, grammar, writing conventions, language use, and vocabulary.

Revising and Editing Workbooks
Students improve language and writing skills by identifying and correcting errors in examples of student writing.

Language Skills Workbooks
Focused exercises on specific language skills including idioms, synonyms, and homophones.

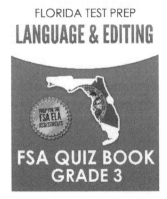 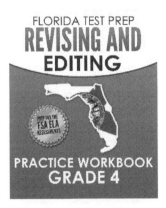 

Made in the
USA
Monee, IL